Strategies for the Assessment and Teaching of History
A Handbook for Secondary Teachers

Carol White

LONGMAN

Acknowledgements

I am grateful to Dr John Fines for the idea of the contract book. I have tried it with students at Garth Hill school following the AEB 630 and ETHOS syllabuses and can testify to its effectiveness.

I would also like to express my thanks to the Humberside teachers who developed the model for the formative record case study on p.54.

Short extracts have been taken from: Purnell, *History of the Twentieth Century*, BPC Publishing Ltd 1969; Andrew Sinclair, *Prohibition*, 1962; B. W. Beacroft and M. A. Smale, *The Making of America*, Longman 1972; I. Leighton (ed), *The Aspirin Age*, Simon and Schuster 1949; R Hofstadter *et al*, *The American Republic Since 1865*, Prentice Hall 1959; Seebohm Rowntree, *Poverty: A Study of Town Life*, Stanley Thorne 1901.

We are grateful to the following for permission to reproduce photographs: Culver pictures, p.17; Hulton-Deutsch Collection, p.31; Imperial War Museum, London, p.9; David King Collection, p.8 left and right; *Punch*, p.32; Topham Picture Source, p.19.
Front Cover: The National Gallery

We are unable to trace the copyright holder of the Rasputin cartoon on p.10 and would appreciate receiving any information that would enable us to do so.

ISBN 0 582 05933 X

First published 1992

Set in Garamond and Sabon

Printed and prepared for publication by Longman York Publishing Services

Contents

Introduction

Assessment of pupils' achievements has always been an integral and fundamental part of teaching. Teachers are constantly making judgments about pupils both in terms of their academic attainment and, with more emphasis recently, in relation to general skills, competences and attitudes. However, although we have accepted, almost without question, the need to make these judgments, we have not always been critically aware of the evidence on which they are based.

In the past few years, as with so much else in education, there has been something of a revolution in attitudes towards assessment; in particular a growing awareness that if statements of assessment are to mean anything to pupils, parents and teachers themselves, they must be derived from evidence which is clear, objective and justifiable.

As far as the teaching of history is concerned, it was the identification of the GCSE national assessment criteria which brought home to most teachers the need for an assessment system in which objectives had been clearly identified and defined and in which assessment tasks were devised which focused on these specific objectives. This preoccupation with assessment objectives continues to dominate as we have moved towards records of achievement, profiling and of course, the National Curriculum.

In the eyes of many teachers however, assessment seems to be in danger of dominating and even distorting the curriculum. In the current debate about the National Curriculum, uppermost in teachers' minds is the composition of the SAT (standard assessment test) and a perception that the externally devised and moderated SAT will be the determining factor to such an extent that it will undermine the teacher's own assessment of pupil achievement and threatens to dictate styles and strategies of teaching and learning.

If the SAT demands a detailed knowledge of dates, events and people across a wide spectrum of programmes of study, this, in turn could lead to didactic and superficial styles of teaching and learning. Teaching to the test could dominate.

It is easy to sympathise with such fears of an assessment-dominated curriculum in which assessment is perceived as the black cloud looming at the end of a course of study, threatening to engulf, to distort and destroy any worthwhile teaching and learning, but are they necessary or well founded?

Most history teachers agree that the influence of the Schools History Project, in particular the impact it had on the definition of the national assessment criteria for GCSE and the application of those criteria to all GCSE history syllabuses, has led to major improvements in the teaching and learning of history 14–16. Mindless recall of facts has been replaced by developing understanding of causation, change, using and evaluating evidence, seeking to understand the perspectives of people in the past (which most teachers still maintain is and should be possible!). In other words, knowledge has replaced factual recall and has led to greater historical understanding. Most history teachers also agree that such developments have also started to have an impact on the junior secondary curriculum and, potentially, on the 16–19 curriculum.

These developments are largely the result of GCSE, and GCSE is a form of assessment, which moreover has been externally imposed, and is at least fifty per cent, (usually more) externally examined. Furthermore, GCSE has been for the most part welcomed by teachers because it is perceived that its impact in the classroom, on the teaching and learning of history, has been beneficial.

Of course there have been problems. There is still some tendency to regard coursework as something extra, over and above the other demands of the course. Many teachers still experience difficulties with levels-of-response mark schemes and with differentiation by outcome. It is not always easy to identify and target specific assessment objectives, but we must remember that GCSE is only a few years old. Indeed, the growing preoccupation with the National Curriculum is likely to swamp GCSE. As I shall discuss further in Chapter 1, we are in grave danger of being lulled into the feeling that we have 'done' GCSE, when in fact what we should be doing is learning from the GCSE experience which relates closely and directly to the proposals in the National Curriculum.

Is it such a terrible thing then to be 'assessment-led'? It depends on the type and style of assessment, and most importantly on how far assessment is regarded and has truly become an integral part of teaching and learning.

Valid and reliable assessment of a pupil's achievement in history cannot be achieved by a 'bolt-on' test which bears little or no relation to what has been going on in the classroom for the rest of the time. Revision for a test on the past week's, month's or year's work is a meaningless activity in itself and such a test will elicit little evidence beyond memory capability, unless the purpose, that is the objective, has been clearly defined and been made clear throughout the teaching. There is little point in teaching one thing and testing something else – and what should be both taught, learned and assessed is historical understanding.

It is also important to consider *the purpose* as well as *the nature* of assessment. Recent work in records of achievement has done a great deal to define and recognise the purpose of assessment as both formative and summative. In particular, if we are to develop strategies by which teachers can acquire the evidence on which informed assessment judgments, both formative and summative, can be made, we must have regard to progression in historical understanding. It is no longer, and arguably never was, a case of 'doing evidence' or of 'skills v. content' but of recognising how historical understanding might develop; and here, as was noted by the Final Report of the National Curriculum History Working Group, we are faced with the fact that to date there has been very little research on progression of historical understanding (DES, 1990).

What experience has told us is that such progression is not linear, that a child does not move ever upward and onward in a straight line. Would that were the case! What we do know is that progression in historical understanding is based on a complex relationship of skills, concepts and context, that the skills and concepts need to be revisited through a number of contexts, that reinforcement is constantly necessary and that, as they do progress, children are able to make wider and more elliptical connections, to handle a broader and deeper knowledge base, to make sense of a growing number of anomalies and seemingly loose ends. What we also suspect is that for too long we have considerably underestimated what children can do by making assumptions about their understanding, based on no hard evidence and a large number of theoretical assumptions.

If such progression, problematic as it is, is to be assessed, it must be monitored throughout the course and not in a 'big bang' at the end. Assessment must be embedded in the whole process of teaching and learning. Any assumption that National Curriculum attainment targets are purely an assessment tool which is somehow different in kind from teaching and learning objectives and that assessment in the National Curriculum is only about testing what pupils know at the end of one or more units of work, can threaten to distort the teaching and learning process and isolate assessment from that process. Best practice at GCSE is now telling us that such isolation need not and should not happen. With the implementation of National Curriculum history, integration of assessment with teaching and learning is a matter of common sense and survival as well as an affirmation of what should be taking place.

Of course there must be monitoring of pupils' achievements. Of course teachers must be able to produce objective, valid and reliable evidence of a pupil's progress – evidence which can be used to inform pupils and their parents where they are now, to develop strategies to help pupils achieve their fullest potential and which can help teachers to evaluate their own strategies. This is the purpose of assessment; but it must be integral to the whole process, embedded within it so that it does not lead or distort what should be taking place in the classroom.

To many teachers, particularly those whose experience includes much time and thought on assessment, this book will contain some suggestions which are already familiar. However, I hope it will reaffirm the conviction that we should be building on and developing good practice. For other teachers, perhaps newer to the profession, assessment does present many challenges. I hope that these ideas and comments, based on my own classroom practice and experience and that of colleagues, will prove useful, as least as a starting point.

I have deliberately started with GCSE and not the National Curriculum, believing that future good practice is built on experience – and GCSE has already provided a good seedbed. It is worth analysing that experience to see how we can use it most effectively for all pupils.

1
GCSE and assessment

Coursework

Since the inception of GCSE, it has constantly been affirmed and reaffirmed that coursework should reflect normal, good classroom practice. Coursework is subject to the same assessment criteria as the written examination, although most examination groups have identified certain specific criteria, most notably 'perspectives of people in the past' as being more suited to be assessed through coursework rather than through examination. Coursework therefore should hold no surprises either for teacher or student. As far as the student in concerned, the coursework component of the GCSE should not make any demands which would not normally be made in terms of time, process, outcome, or means of assessment. In preparing pupils for GCSE, teachers will devise a range of tasks, a small number of which will be identified as the formal coursework component. Ideally, these coursework tasks which will be focused on the same assessment objectives as other assignments, should not differ substantially in any kind or dimension from other tasks set during the course and should thus be regarded as totally integral to the teaching, learning and assessment process of GCSE.

Coursework – at home or in class?

There has been considerable debate about whether coursework is best designed to be done at home or in the classroom. There is the argument that, given an examination which carries sixty to seventy per cent of the final GCSE weighting, it is not unreasonable to give students the opportunity to show what they can do by themselves when they have time to research and write at leisure.

There are, however, difficulties. Some students produce high quality work, but have clearly spent far longer than was intended, thus adding to the perceived overload of coursework which was so vocally criticised during the first run through of GCSE in 1986–1988. Moreover, it is apparent that some students do receive considerable help and guidance from home, ranging from access to a wide variety of reference materials to parents who are willing and able to give time, support and, in some cases, considerably more to ensure a good result in coursework, thus once again compounding the belief that coursework is 'special'. Conversely, other students, because of their home situation, do not and cannot receive this sort of support.

The following strategy avoids the unfair discrimination and at the same time does allow coursework to develop naturally from what is happening in the classroom.

1. All students are given the same task and work within the same structure.
2. All students are given the same sources from which they are expected to work. Thus, no students are expected to 'find out' for themselves and so will not be disadvantaged because they do not have access to the reference materials. (The one exception to this is where it is the process of an investigation which is being assessed rather than the outcome; where what is being assessed is the student's ability to take part in a historical enquiry. This, however, is not common practice at present in GCSE.)
3. Part at least of the coursework is done in class; thus, it is easier to ensure that what is being produced is the student's own work and that it arises naturally out of what has been going on in the classroom. The task is explained and started in the lesson, the source booklet or worksheet is discussed, any difficulties in comprehension dealt with and the students required to work in silence, on their own. If necessary, they may finish the assignment for homework, and homework time may be set aside for completion. It must be made clear, however, that this is not something over and above normal homework and the assignment is not intended to take more time than the usual homework allocation.
4. An alternative approach, if time allows, is to give a generous classtime allocation which will allow the slowest workers adequate time. Extra tasks should be planned involving extension work for the more able and a range of alternatives for those who work quickly but whose approach tends to be superficial. Every encouragement, however, should be given to these pupils to reconsider their work in order to ensure that they have answered as fully as possibly – a point which must be borne in mind when constructing the task.
5. Students should be told in advance how much classtime and homework has been allocated and what length is expected.

Experience suggests that this format works reasonably well, and does keep a perspective in the minds of both students and teachers about the relationship between coursework and classwork. However, the distinction will continue to exist while pupils realise that teachers also regard coursework as 'different' and while the handling of coursework is seen to be different from that of normal classwork.

Coursework as normal practice

There are a number of ways in which coursework can be integrated more fully into the normal classroom practice. Ian Colwill and Maureen Burns have suggested a number of useful strategies developed by teachers at the History and Social Science Teachers' Centre where examples of planning grids can be used to ensure that coursework is planned and integrated in the scheme of work from the start and is not an afterthought designed at the end of the course purely to satisfy the requirements of the Boards (Colwill and Burns, 1989).

One obvious strategy, widely adopted, is to integrate coursework throughout the course and not, as was frequently the case first time round, to expect students to do all their coursework at the end of the course or at least in Year 11. Apart from anything else, sheer pressure of work on both students and teachers has ensured that coursework assignments now tend to be more evenly distributed.

Furthermore, when Boards require only two or three pieces of coursework, there is again the quite understandable tendency to avoid doing more than is required. If so few pieces are produced, this only serves to enhance the separate nature of coursework. To be a true reflection of classwork, it should be possible to submit samples of work done throughout the GCSE course which arise naturally from what is taking place in class.

It could be argued that separate character of coursework was emphasised by the original requirement of some GCSE Boards to validate proposed coursework assignments and mark schemes in advance. The requirement now seems to be declining and was clearly perceived by the Boards as part of the GCSE learning curve while teachers were getting to grips with the implications of defined assessment criteria and differentiation by outcome. Nor is that learning process complete. We are very far from have 'done' GCSE but have gained considerably in expertise and confidence. Over the last few years, schools have started to co-operate and to share in the production of assignments. Support cluster groups have begun to produce a range of assignments which can be used both as coursework assessments and as useful exercises within the classroom. After all, the assessment criteria are the same both for coursework and the examination and most Boards do not discriminate in the content requirements between coursework and the examination. The indications are, that with growing confidence and expertise in developing such units, teachers are becoming increasingly adept at devising a range of assessment tasks, focused on the assessment criteria, which are able to differentiate by outcome and which can therefore be used where most appropriate as classwork, homework or coursework.

For the time being, though, the belief that GCSE coursework is different both in kind from 'normal' work and certainly in the way it is assessed and moderated does still prevail. There is the perception that more effort is required in the devising and presentation of coursework assignments: indeed a number of Chief Examiners and Chief Moderators have remarked at how much effort teachers have put into coursework assignments and have intimated that such effort if not misplaced, is certainly unnecessary. In order to do justice to themselves and their students, some teachers have spent hours in the presentation of source booklets and worksheets and in devising assignment of inordinate length. It is not necessary to produce such a *magnum opus* in order to satisfy the coursework requirements, nor to meet the National Criteria.

Planned coursework assessment

The key to integrated coursework assessment with the teaching and learning of GCSE must be in the planning. As already noted, Colwill and Burns discuss matrix planning as a useful way forward and the key to that is to define what is to be assessed at the same time as planning what is to be taught and learned.

Case study: Planning a coursework assignment

Assessment objective: Evaluation of evidence
Unit of work: The Russian Revolution, 1917
Topic: The use of film as a source of evidence

This model was devised by a group of teachers in Berkshire to be used with pupils following a Modern World GCSE syllabus.

Students had been studying a unit of work on the Russian Revolution. They were familiar with the events of the 1917 Revolutions and were now considering a variety of accounts of what took place. It was also felt at this stage that they should become aware of the 'mythic' dimensions of the Russian Revolution. It was decided to explore the very powerful use of film as a source of evidence for the Revolution and to try to make students aware that film, as much as any written source, is liable to bias and distortion. We were concerned that students who would interrogate written sources with an informed scepticism tended to regard the film of *Doctor Zhivago* as the definitive version of the events of the Russian Revolution!

The coursework exercise was planned to take place over a two-week period, during which the pupils watched extracts from *Doctor Zhivago,* Eisenstein's *October* and from a television documentary, *Ten Days that Shook the World,* which used extracts of the Eisenstein film as if it were newsreel footage.

The exercise was devised by a group of teachers who had formed themselves into a support cluster group, preparing pupils for the same GCSE Modern World syllabus. The various films were edited on to one tape which was then copied so that all schools had a copy and the teaching strategy and questions to be asked were devised by the group working together.

The extracts were relatively short, five minutes at most, and interspersed with discussion, groupwork and coursework tasks which were started in class, following from the activity which arose out of watching the film extracts, and finished at home.

Over two weeks the students developed a piece of coursework, with a series of structured tasks which arose naturally out of the parallel classroom activity, and the emphasis should be on 'parallel', rather than at the end of the unit.

Integrating assessment tasks

Many teachers have used a modular structure to organise their GCSE courses. Indeed, with the considerable reduction in content and the identification of a manageable number of content areas, such a course structure makes a great deal of sense. However, there can be problems if the dependence on the end-of-module assessment becomes too doctrinaire and if it is assumed that coursework can be done only through such assessments.

Obviously, if it is outcome rather than process which is being assessed, the pupils must have had the opportunity to develop their knowledge, skills and understanding of a particular unit of work, but this does not necessarily mean that the whole unit of work must be complete before such an assessment can take place. The following case study provides an example.

Case study: A structured coursework assignment

Assessment objective: Cause and consequence
Unit of work: The Russian Revolutions, 1917–24
Topic: The causes of the 1917 Revolution

Any study of the Russian Revolution will entail discussion of the causes of what took place in 1917. Students will need to consider the broad range of causes, long and short term. They should be given the opportunity to consider their relative importance and, ultimately, to reach an informed decision, which they are able to explain and support with evidence about the major factors which explain the overthrow of the Tsar in 1917.

This case study provides a structure which demonstrates how a coursework assignment, designed to assess GCSE Assessment Objective 2, 'cause and consequence', not only arises naturally from the teaching and learning of the topic but also can be fully integrated within what is happening in the classroom.

Section 1: Living and working conditions

Sources 1A and 1B are photographs of poor Russian peasants in 1912.

[1A] A homeless beggar

[1B] Barge haulers pulling a barge along the river Volga

1. *What evidence is there from these pictures that these men are poor?*
2. *How might industrial development have improved the life and work of the people in these photographs?*
3. *How might the First World War have made life even more difficult for these men and their families?*

COMMENT

These questions could be the basis for a group discussion in which they were considered and responses reported back to the whole class. It is important that, following such discussions, the teacher emphasises the main points, especially if a follow-up piece of coursework is intended, so that all pupils will have the opportunity to appreciate important issues which may need to be picked up later.

> Wages are being reduced. Rent allowances and bonuses are being taken away. Hours of work are being extended. Workers who make trouble are blacklisted. The system of fines and beating up is in full swing.

[1C] From Joseph Stalin's diary, describing conditions in an industrial town in 1901

COMMENT

We know a great deal about Joseph Stalin after 1924, but what position did he hold in 1917? Since no source should be accepted as given, students should be encouraged to ask questions about the author of the source which might explain a particular standpoint or point of view. The revolutionary activities of young Stalin therefore have a direct bearing on this source.

4. *Was life in the town any easier? Use source 1C to explain your answer.*

Section 2: Russia and the First World War

Students will have studied the economic and social conditions in Russia before 1914. They will, also have spent some time considering the role and position of the Tsar, the social structure, maybe the 1905 Revolution and the growing political unrest. This assignment does not attempt to include all these aspects but is focusing on some of the areas which will have been covered in the unit.

Students are now asked to consider the impact of the war on Russia. In 1914, Russia entered the war against Germany and Austria. By 1915, the Russian army had been defeated and was in retreat.

> In recent battles, a third of the men had no rifles. The poor devils had to wait until their comrades fell before their eyes and they could pick up weapons.

[2A] Extract from a Russian general's diary, 1914

In the summer of 1915, nearly, 1,500,000 officers and men were taken prisoner.

[2B] A photograph of Russian prisoners of war with their weapons, 1915

1. *From the evidence given in sources 2A and 2B, how do you think many Russian soldiers would have felt in 1916*
a) *about the war;*
b) *about the Tsar and his government?*
   In your groups, use the sources to give reasons for your answers. Use the evidence in the sources to back up what you are saying.

2. *Work on this question with your neighbour and write your answer in your book.*
a) *By 1917, how did many Russians who were not fighting in the war feel about the Tsar and his government?*
b) *Why did so many soldiers desert from the army?*
   Use the sources we have just looked at. Also think back to the extract from Doctor Zhivago which we watched.

Section 3: Rasputin

Having considered the general impact of the war, the pupils now turn their attention to the influence of Rasputin over Nicholas and Alexandra and consider how far that influence was a factor in the downfall of the Tsar.

[3A] A cartoon of Rasputin with Nicholas and Alexandra, 1915

1. *What do you think the cartoonist is trying to say about Rasputin? Use the cartoon to explain your answer.*
2. *When people looked at this cartoon, can you suggest what they would think about Nicholas and Alexandra?*

Having used these sources to consider three possible causes for the 1917 Revolution, pupils are now led towards a synthesis of this work and to consider the question which is also to be assessed as a coursework assignment.

1. *These sources have looked at aspects of the causes of the Russian Revolution: the living conditions of many of the people, the effect of the First World War on Russia, the influence of Rasputin on the Royal Family.*
   Which of these causes do you think was the most important? Rank them so that 1 = highest; 3 = lowest). Explain why you have put them in this order.

Assignment

Would the Russian Revolution have taken place in 1917 if Russia had not been involved in the First World War?

POINTS TO REMEMBER

- consider all the causes you have looked at;
- think about your order of importance and the reasons you gave for it;
- you are not just writing about the war, but about the other causes as well;
- aim for about 700–1000 words and use the sources to explain the points you make.

COMMENT

Pupils have been led into this assignment through a structure of questions. With the assignment they have also been given indicators of what is expected. Does this distort the outcome and give too much help? The following mark scheme demonstrates that a range of responses can still be elicited and experience has shown that such guidance does not constitute undue help or spoon-feeding.

The ladder of access produced by such a structure can, though frequent use in class, demonstrate to pupils how such questions might be unpacked, but there will always be those who remain on the lowest rungs of the ladder. Such structure, as will be demonstrated throughout this chapter, is not only essential in framing an assignment but is also a key strategy in providing the greatest access to the widest range of ability.

MARK SCHEME

Level 1
Partial narrative with little explicit identification of the causal link between the war and the Revolution.

Level 2
Explanation of the effects of the war on Russia. Identifies specific causal link between war and revolution but not in the general context of other causes.

Level 3
Identifies and explains a range of causes of the Revolution.

Level 4
Identifies and explains a hierarchy of importance of causes.

Level 5
Perceives and explains the war as the catalyst for revolution.

NOTES ON THE CASE STUDY
A number of general points arise from this proposed mark scheme.

1. How many levels? Despite the impression given by some GCSE moderators and Boards, this does not have to be, and indeed should not be, perceived as a predetermined number. The number of levels for coursework must be flexible and should depend on the nature of the assignment. However, some Boards do seem to assume that three is a desirable number of levels, and certainly frame their examination with this in mind.

2. When moderating the candidate's work (post hoc moderation), if no candidate reaches the highest level, what is to be done? If specified mark bands are associated with particular levels, this could be an issue, and it is not one on which at present there is any consensus among the Boards. If in doubt, check before you assume that you can reallocate the marks – or it may be a case of redefining the levels statement.

3. There is also the vexed question of sustaining a response at a particular level. Agreement does now seem to have been reached that a response must show a sustained level of understanding for credit to be given and that the 'flash in the pan' response does not count. Of course, if the assignment is broken down into a number of short questions, it is possible for a candidate to respond at a variety of levels, but in a longer piece of work the response must be sustained if the level is to be given.

Marking coursework differently

Assessment at GCSE, for both coursework and the examination, is based on differentiation by outcome. Many teachers still shy away from levels-of-response marking because it is regarded as time consuming, 'marking everything twice'. It is therefore often the case that levels mark schemes are produced for coursework assignments to be submitted but are not used as a normal and regular means of assessment. Thus the language of 'levels' is not the common vocabulary of assessment used by teachers to pupils, which serves yet again to reinforce the separateness of coursework.

In May 1988, SEAC produced *Differentiation by Outcome in History*, a report by SEC/Joint Council Working Party, designed to give advice and guidance to history examiners on the creation of questions and mark schemes which did succeed in differentiating by outcome. This report, although directed at examiners, provides very useful guidelines for teachers devising coursework assignments and mark schemes which can be differentiated by outcome. This report was followed by the Report of the Chief Examiners in History which also contains useful papers on differentiation by outcome (SEAC, 1989). Furthermore, despite the shifting sands of these rapidly changing times, the guidance still holds good as we move from GCSE towards National Curriculum assessment.

Figure 1 is an adaptation of the diagram produced in *Differentiation by Outcome in History* which displays the stages of development of a written examination question. This can be made to apply equally to the construction not only of an assignment to be submitted as coursework but also of any assignment, since it is a description of good practice.

Fig. 1
The written exam
question

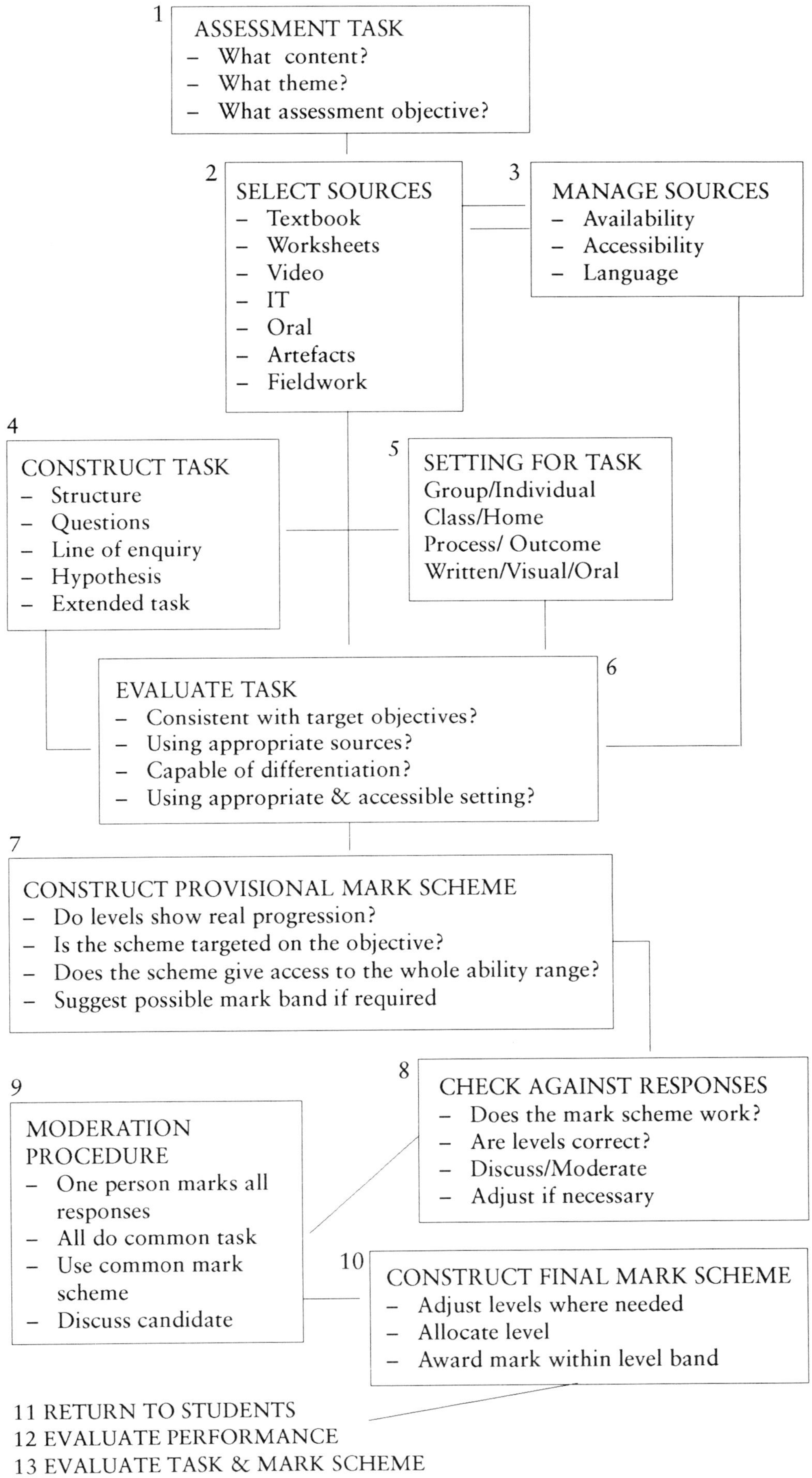

1 | ASSESSMENT TASK
- What content?
- What theme?
- What assessment objective?

2 | SELECT SOURCES
- Textbook
- Worksheets
- Video
- IT
- Oral
- Artefacts
- Fieldwork

3 | MANAGE SOURCES
- Availability
- Accessibility
- Language

4 | CONSTRUCT TASK
- Structure
- Questions
- Line of enquiry
- Hypothesis
- Extended task

5 | SETTING FOR TASK
Group/Individual
Class/Home
Process/ Outcome
Written/Visual/Oral

6 | EVALUATE TASK
- Consistent with target objectives?
- Using appropriate sources?
- Capable of differentiation?
- Using appropriate & accessible setting?

7 | CONSTRUCT PROVISIONAL MARK SCHEME
- Do levels show real progression?
- Is the scheme targeted on the objective?
- Does the scheme give access to the whole ability range?
- Suggest possible mark band if required

8 | CHECK AGAINST RESPONSES
- Does the mark scheme work?
- Are levels correct?
- Discuss/Moderate
- Adjust if necessary

9 | MODERATION PROCEDURE
- One person marks all responses
- All do common task
- Use common mark scheme
- Discuss candidate

10 | CONSTRUCT FINAL MARK SCHEME
- Adjust levels where needed
- Allocate level
- Award mark within level band

11 RETURN TO STUDENTS
12 EVALUATE PERFORMANCE
13 EVALUATE TASK & MARK SCHEME

Case study: Checklist for designing assignments

1. *The task*
   - What content is to be assessed?
   - Is this part of a thematic approach? If so, what is the relationship to the theme?
   - What is the assessment objective?

2. *The sources*
   - What sources will be used in the assignment?

3. *Accessibility*
   - Check for accessibility: language, clarity, availability for all students, presentation.

4. *Constructing the task*
   - Does it have a structure (see below)?
   - Open/closed questions: hypothesis testing, line of enquiry, extended task, focused on process or outcome?

5. *Setting for task*
   - Group work/individual assignment:
     - in class/at home;
     - written, visual, oral;
     - time allocated.

6. *Evaluate task*
   - Does it focus on the intended objective?
   - Are the sources appropriate?
   - Is task sufficiently open-ended to allow for differentiation?
   - Is the setting appropriate for the task and accessible to pupils?

7. *Construct provisional mark scheme*
   - Is the scheme targeted on the assessment objective?
   - Do levels show real progression?
   - Does the scheme give access to the whole ability range?
   - Suggest possible mark band, if required.

8. *Pupils complete the assignment*

9. *Mark assignment following guidelines of mark scheme*
   - Does scheme work?
   - Are levels appropriate?
   - Note inconsistencies.

10. *Moderation*
    - How has assignment been marked?
      Moderation can be achieved by one person marking assignment for all students.
    - All pupils have completed a common assignment with a common mark scheme.
    - Responses are discussed and, if necessary mark scheme adjusted.
    - Adjust mark bands if necessary.

11. *Return work to students*
- Share mark scheme.
- Discuss levels.
- Individual/group advice to help to move to higher level.

12. *Evaluate performance*
- Record/report attainment in mark book/record of achievement/profile.

13. *Evaluate test and mark scheme*

Listed like this, the task seems monumental, yet this is what many teachers are doing, and, since the advent of GCSE, have done so often that much of it has become second nature. Furthermore, the further this process is embedded in what takes place during teaching and learning, the less of an additional extra it becomes. Common sense also dictates that this entire process does not take place every time we design an assignment. However, we should accept that early attempts at coursework and levels-of-response mark schemes do need to be evaluated and good practice should lead us to engage in a cycle of evaluation and adaptation.

Targeting objectives

Single-objective assignments

The issue of single-objective assignments is still somewhat contentious. Since 1990, most examining groups have either strongly advised or actually insisted on single-objective assessment in GCSE coursework. It can be argued that such an approach to setting coursework, or indeed examination questions, distorts the study of history which should not be divided into separate assessment boxes. It is not easy to separate objectives and in doing so, surely undue emphasis is given to a single component within a complex study. For example, in a piece of coursework on the role of the French Resistance in the Second World War, the targeted objective was the role of an individual or movement in a historical context. Attention was focused on the contribution of the French Resistance to the planning behind the Normandy Landings, especially on the information they passed on about the Atlantic Wall and the German defences. Whilst planning the assignment and selecting appropriate sources, it became increasingly difficult to separate the role of a particular group from more general causation questions about D-Day. Issues of motivation were also clearly involved, as was the validity and reliability of the evidence.

All questions devised were appropriate, relevant and important historical questions and we felt restricted and constrained by the demand for a single-objective assignment. There was a growing feeling that what we were asking the students to do was contrived and would not necessarily contribute towards their understanding of the reasons for the success of the D-Day landings. Thus, was the assessment requirement working against our attempts to help our students increase their historical understanding? It was at this point that we realised that we were in danger of letting our preoccupation with assessment take over and distort our teaching. We were starting to 'teach to test' rather than to use the assessment objectives to help us to identify for the purpose of that particular assessment assignment on which area of historical understanding we were focusing.

Single-objective assignments are problematic but are a necessary part of the teacher's learning process as far as assessment is concerned. If this approach is not adopted, assessment and indeed planning for teaching and learning, can become vague and lacking in direction. If the assignment is targeted on one objective, it is necessary to plan the task with that objective in mind. It follows that we must select sources to fit the objective rather than contrive an assignment around a variety of sources which we have taken a lot of time and effort to find and are determined to use at any cost, however appropriate they may be to a particular assignment.

Recent good practice at GCSE has demonstrated that the GCSE criteria are not to be regarded just as objectives for assessment purposes but lie at the heart of the overall planning of a history course. Indeed, if the assessment objectives are valid, they must identify what constitutes understanding in history and therefore should be integral to the whole teaching and learning process, and this must be the way forward in the teaching, learning and assessment of the National Curriculum.

Targeting single objectives is a necessary part of the learning curve for setting and marking GCSE coursework. Just as SEAC encourages Chief Examiners to set questions in which the targeted objective is clear and identified to the candidates, so teachers should adopt the same approach in devising coursework assignments. As a first step, to help clarify the process of focusing on defined objectives, the single-objective assignment would seem to be a sensible approach. With growing expertise and confidence, it should then be possible to move towards assignments which focus on more than one objective, although, as discussed below, I would still maintain that the most effective way to tackle multi-objective assignments is through separate questions within the same assessment tasks. Expertise in this approach has been further developed in such syllabuses as NEA, SHP Mode 2 and the LEAG Modern World modular syllabus.

Case study: A single-objective assignment

Assessment objective: Perspectives of people in the past
Unit of work: The Prohibition era in the United States

Comment

Of all the GCSE national criteria, the objective designed to assess the perspectives of people in the past has achieved the most notoriety. One reason why the empathy objective has received such a bad press – from many teachers as well as the media – is a lack of clarity about the objective itself and the fear that it might lead to uncontrolled flights of fancy which have little to do with the rigorous discipline of history. This fear seems to have been placed in a largely misguided belief that empathy exercises should not be subject to the same disciplined rules of evidence as other areas of historical debate and that 'what might have been' or 'imagine you are' belongs to fairy tales and not to the study of history.

Once again, structured questions can be a useful way of linking the sources and the empathetic exercise to ensure that the response is based on sound historical evidence.

Context

This assignment derives from a study which has already been undertaken on the Prohibition era in the United States. The structured questions guide pupils through the sources and help them to select what might be relevant and helpful for their response to the question which is focused on a single objective: the perspectives of people in the past.

SLAVES OF THE SALOON

The saloon business cannot exist without slaves. You may smile at that statement, but it is absolutely true. Is not the man who is addicted to the drink habit a slave? There are 1,000,000 such slaves in the United States. They are slaves of the saloon. They go out and work a week or a month, draw their pay, go into the saloon, and hand the saloon keeper their money for something which ruins their own lives. Is not this slavery? Has there ever been in the history of the world a worse system of slavery? It is quite natural, of course, that the slaveholder should not care to liberate these slaves.— *Richmond P. Hobson.*

A woman entered a barroom, and advanced quietly to her husband, who sat drinking with three other men. "Thinkin' ye'd be too busy to come home to supper, Jack, I've fetched it to you here."
And she departed. The man laughed awkwardly. He invited his friends to share the meal with him. Then he removed the cover from the dish. The dish was empty. It contained a slip of paper that said: "I hope you will enjoy your supper. It is the same your wife and children have at home."-- *Chicago Chronicle.*

The liquor traffic, like the slave trade or piracy, cannot be mended, and therefore must be actually ended.—*Joseph Cook.*

[A] A poster produced by the Anti-Saloon League, 1910

> Bolshevism flourishes in wet soil. Failure to enforce prohibition in Russian was followed by Bolshevism.
>
> Failure to enforce Prohibition HERE will encourage disrespect for law and INVITE INDUSTRIAL DISASTER.
>
> Radical and Bolshevist outbreaks are practically unknown in states where Prohibition has been in effect for years. Bolshevism live on booze.

[B] From a poster displayed by the Nashville Tennessee chapter of the Anti-Saloon league

The Anti-Saloon League was a religious organisation which wanted to ban the sale of alcoholic drinks throughout the United States. In 1917, America entered the war against Germany. This helped the Anti-Saloon League as many American breweries were run by German immigrants.

Pabst and Bucsh (major brewing firms) were German, therefore beer was unpatriotic. Liquor stopped American soldiers from firing straight therefore liquor was a total evil. Brewing used up 11 million loaves of barley a day which could have fed the starving allies, therefore consumption of alcohol was treason.

[C] From *Prohibition* by Andrew Sinclair, 1962

Source D is an extract from a relatively recent history textbook. In this extract the authors sum up the effects of Prohibition.

> Prohibition was intended to stop the liquor trade, drunkenness and crime in the towns and cities. It failed in this aim. Most Americans ignored the law, Alcohol prices rocketed upwards, supplies fell and drunkenness declined, but Americans did not stop drinking. Some American cities became even more corrupt . . . The manufacture and sale of alcohol fell into the hands of bootleggers, moonshiners, rumrunners, hi-jackers, gangsters, racketeers, gunmen and speakeasy operators. The bootleggers sold redistilled industrial alcohol, the moonshiners made their own home brews, and the rumrunner smuggled liquor into American by ship, speedboat, car and lorry from Europe, the West Indies, Canada and Mexico. The hi-jackers were modern highway-men who stole the alcohol laden boats, cars, and lorries of the bootleggers and the rumrunners who soon hired professional gunmen to protect their interests. Every city and town contained its speakeasies where alcohol was sold illegally to customers who quietly spoke the right passwords at the door. Gangsters operated protection rackets to shield those in the trade. Many judges and policemen not only received bribes from gangsters and racketeers but were bootleggers, moonshiners and rumrunners themselves. Some operators made millions of dollars profit from the illegal alcohol trade. They have been called the barons of booze. It is not surprising to learn that the 1920s has also been labelled 'the Lawless Decade'.

[D] From *The Making of America* by B. W. Bearcroft and M. A. Smale, 1972

Source E, is also taken from a recent history book.

> Chicago in 1925 . . . had 16,000 more arrests for drunkenness than England and Wales. By 1927 drunken driving offences had risen by 467%, deaths from alcoholism 600% on the 1920 level. In a single year of Prohibition the United States consumed 200 million gallons of hard liquor, 685 million gallons of malt liquor and 118 million gallons of wine. By 1932, 2,000 civilians across the country, mainly gangsters and allied beer runners had been killed 'in action' and 500 Prohibition agents ended in their graves unexpectedly . . . The Great Crash and the Depression dried up the torrent of money flowing into the coffers of organised crime and provided the climate in which Prohibition and all its works could be finally discredited.

[E] From Purnell's *History of the Twentieth Century,* 1969

The Government tried to stop the making, selling and drinking of alcohol by appointing 'prohibition agents'. One of the best-known was Izzy Einstein. A journalist, Herbert Asbury used stories about Izzy in New York newspapers of the time to give him the material for his account of Izzy's work.

> Izzy's first assignment was to clean up a place in Brooklyn which the enforcement authorities shrewdly suspected housed a 'speakeasy', since drunken men has been seen staggering from the building and the air for half a block around was full with fumes of beer and whisky. Several agents had snooped and slunk around the house but none had been able to get inside. Izzy knew nothing of detective procedures; he simply walked up to the joint and knocked on the door. A peephole was opened and a hoarse voice demanded to know who was there.

> 'Izzy Einstein,' said Izzy, 'I want a drink'. 'O yeah? Who sent you here, bud, What's you business?'

> 'My boss sent me,' Izzy explained. 'I'm a prohibition agent. I just got appointed.'

> The door swung open and the doorman slapped Izzy jovially on the back.

'Ho! Ho!' he cried, 'Come right in, bud. That's the best gag I've heard yet.'

Izzy stepped into a room where half a dozen men were drinking at a small make-shift bar.

'Hey boss!' the doorman yelled, 'Here's a prohibition agent wants a drink! You got a badge too bud?'

'Sure I have,' said Izzy, and produced it.

'Well I'm damned' said the man behind the bar, 'Looks just like the real thing.'

He poured a slug of whisky and Izzy downed it. That was a mistake for when the time came to 'make the pinch' Izzy had no evidence. He tried to grab the bottle but the bartender ran out of the back door with it.

'I learned right there,' said Izzy, 'that a slug of hooch [spirits] in an agent's belly might feel good, but it ain't evidence.'

So when he went home that night he rigged up an evidence collector. He put a small funnel in the upper left hand pocket of his vest [waistcoat] and connected it, by means of a rubber tube, with a flat bottle concealed in the lining of the garment. Thereafter when a drink was served to him, Izzy took a small sip, then poured the remainder into the funnel while the bartender was making change [at the till]. There was always enough for analysis to offer in evidence.

'I'd have died if it hadn't been for that little funnel and the bottle' said Izzy, 'most of the stuff I got in those places was terrible.'

[F] From *The Aspirin Age 1919–41* edited by I. Leighton, 1949

The most powerful of the gangs involved in bootlegging was led by Al Capone. By 1927, Capone was earning $60 million a year. He had 700 men under his command and one by one, his rivals were killed. The most famous gangland killing was the St Valentine's Day Massacre in 1929 when seven members of the Bugs Moran gang were gunned down by Capone's men. Capone made no secret of his activities but was able to get away with crime because he has Chicago's police and politicians in his pay. In 1930, 'Public Enemy Number One' made the front cover of *Time* magazine.

[G] From *Time*, Vol. XV, No 12, 1930

I call myself a business man. I make money by supplying a popular demand. If I break the law, my customers are as guilty as I am.

[H] Al Capone from *The Age of Excess* by J. Brooman, 1986

By 1931, it was clear that Prohibition was not working. This poem sums up the problems.

> Prohibition is an awful flop.
>   We like it.
> It can't stop what it's meant to stop.
>   We like it.
> It's left a trail of graft and slime,
> It's filled our land with vice and crime.
> It don't prohibit worth a dime,
>   Nevertheless, we're for it.

[I] From *The American Republic Since 1865* by R. Hofstadter, William Miller and Daniel Aaron, 1959

Assessment assignment: Attitudes towards Prohibition in the USA, 1918–32

In this assignment, you need to think about what the Americans thought about Prohibition, which was introduced in America in 1918 and abolished in 1932.

You have already done quite a lot of work on this topic and should use your notes to help you with this assignment.

You also have a number of sources which have been given to you with the assignment.

Sources A to C give some reasons why some people wanted Prohibition. Sources D to I tell us something about the effects of Prohibition and help us to understand why, by 1932, most Americans wanted it to be abolished.

1. *Look at and read sources A to C carefully. With a partner, list those people who wanted Prohibition and why they wanted it. You should be able to find at least one group of people and reasons from each source.*

2. *Look carefully at sources D to E. With your partner, find at least three pieces of evidence from each source to support the claim that Prohibition led to an increase in crime and violence.*

3. *Read source F carefully. Why do you think that there were several newspaper stories about Izzy Einstein? How do you think readers would have reacted to this story? Use the source to give full reasons for your answer.*

4. *Look at and read sources G and H. Use the sources to explain how people might have felt about Al Capone. Did all people feel the same way about him? Explain your answer fully.*

5. *Read source I carefully. What feeling about Prohibition is summed-up in this poem?*

6. *With a partner, talk about why some people might have been in favour of Prohibition in 1917 and have changed their minds by 1931. Make brief notes of your answers. They should help you in the assignment.*

Now, use your answers to these questions to help you to tackle the following task:

A newspaper editorial published in 1932 is considering the Prohibition issue. The editorial looks at the reasons for the introduction of Prohibition and the effects of the policy. The newspaper editor has strong views about the subject and these are clearly shown in the article. With these comments in mind, write the editorial for the newspaper.

COMMENT

How much help should be given through the initial structure? There is no reason why the 'warm up' questions should not be used as the basis for discussion. After all, it is part of the teaching and learning process to help pupils perceive the link between the sources and the assessment task. It is not comprehension of the sources which is being assessed but understanding of perspectives of people in the past. As part of the teaching of this topic, pupils should be helped to understand the diversity of reactions to Prohibition and the reasons for that diversity. Not all students will achieve the highest levels in their responses – indeed, if that were the case, the task would have failed because it did not differentiate, but too often, pupils do not show what they know, understand and can do, because they do not fully appreciate what it is they are being asked to do. The structure which opens up the assignment is a *teaching strategy* designed to help pupils realise their full potential.

For several twentieth-century topics, critical viewing of feature films can be one way of exploring attitudes and feelings, and, with Attainment Target 2 in mind, could be used as a basis for discussion about film as a medium for presenting history. Sparing and judicious use of *The Untouchables*, for example can have a great impact on this particular topic, especially perceptions about Al Capone.

Pupils can make deductions about attitudes and values from information provided by secondary sources – hence the inclusion of sources E and F.

MARK SCHEME

Level 1

Feelings about Prohibition are shown as being uniform and not supported by evidence.

Level 2

Feelings and attitudes about Prohibition are supported by evidence and shown as being uniform.

Level 3

A diversity of feelings and attitudes towards Prohibition is discussed and supported by evidence.

Level 4

Awareness that attitudes towards Prohibition changed. Gives reasons for these changes, thus demonstrating an understanding of a diversity of reactions in a changing historical context.

Multi-objective assignments

As expertise is gained in targeting and focusing on specific objectives, it is possible to construct tasks which do contain more than one specified objective and thus overcome the danger of distortion and compartmentalisation. There are various ways in which this might be done.

For example, it is of course possible to design a task in which a number of assessment objectives have been identified but which for the purposes of this particular assessment focuses on one specified objective. In the Prohibition case study, for example, the 'warm up' questions could be framed as source evaluation questions but the focus of the assignment for assessment purposes was the empathy objective.

Another approach, often used by teachers in coursework design, sets a range of questions targeted on different objectives. Thus the whole assignment identifies possibly two or three objectives with different questions aimed at different objectives.

Case study: *Multi-objective assignments*

Assessment objectives: Source evaluation and perspectives of people in the past
Unit of work: The Prohibition era in the United States

Take the Prohibition assignment. The target was 'perspectives of people in the past', but the same sources might be used for source evaluation *and* the perspectives of people in the past.

The assignment questions could then be:
1. *Read sources D and E carefully. How do sources F, G, H and I provide evidence for what is said in these sources?*
   (Evidence objective)

2. *Source F is a 'primary' account of what happened during Prohibition. How far is it a valuable source of evidence for what happened during Prohibition?*
   (Evidence objective)

3. *How might an American mother of young children have felt*
   a) *about the introduction of Prohibition in 1918?*
   b) *about the abolition of Prohibition in 1933?*
   (Empathy objective)

MARK SCHEME
Question 1
Below base. Identified points made in D and E without cross-referencing to F, G, H and I.

Level 1
Makes a few general connections without supporting evidence from the sources, i.e. demonstrates comprehension.

Level 2
Makes some connections, supported by evidence from one source, i.e. limited cross reference.

Level 3
Makes a range of connections supported by evidence across the sources, i.e. synthesis.

Level 4

Makes an evaluation of 'how far' the secondary evidence in sources D and E is supported by F, G, H and I, i.e. recognises the gaps as well as the support.

Question 2
Level 1

The sources are useful because it is an eyewitness.

Level 2

Uses evidence from the source to note valuable detail.

Level 3

Recognises value of sources but questions provenance: audience and purpose of the source – newspaper accounts.

Question 3
Level 1

Everyone thought Prohibition was a failure and should never have been introduced.

Level 2

In 1918, there were good reasons for introducing Prohibition (examples given) but these had changed by 1933 (reasons given).

Level 3

Some people wanted Prohibition (identifies who and why), others did not. Explains why attitudes changed during 1920s. Identifies who might still have supported Prohibition in 1933.

Level 4

As level 3 and recognises that those who wanted Prohibition were a minority who lobbied the hardest.

Common assessment for all?

The HMI Report on the first GCSE examination was critical of the accessibility, or lack of it, of the history GCSE examination papers for candidates with reading and writing difficulties. Many teachers agreed. It was felt that, in a number of ways, Chief Examiners and the examination groups could have paid more regard to the difficulties of these candidates and could have produced papers which were less daunting and which would enable them to demonstrate what they knew, understood and could do.

Layout

What was wrong with these papers? The following points provide a useful checklist when constructing coursework for the whole ability range.

1. Instructions must be clear and succinct. For coursework, it is important to spend enough time introducing the assignment in the classroom so that points of difficulty and misunderstanding can be clarified and teachers can spell out exactly what is required. Instructions should be clearly written down even if they have already been explained. Someone's attention may have wandered at the crucial point but at least they can read

what they are supposed to do later! Starting the assignment in class means candidates will not only have to read the instructions but will have started to follow them, have had the opportunity to sort out any initial difficulties and have worked themselves into the 'rhythm' of the assignment.

2. The layout of the assignment should make clear which sources relate to which questions, and allow enough space to break up chunks of text – this can help those with reading difficulties, and be less off-putting.

3. If photocopies of pictures and diagrams are used, pictures should be clear – always a difficult task and one which should be borne in mind when selecting pictures. It is pointless devising an assignment with a marvellous range of colour reproductions which turn into a formless haze when photocopied. Of course, any extracts, pictures and diagrams used in coursework assignments should gain copyright clearance before they are reproduced.

4. *The structure* of the assignment must be clear to the reader. Candidates must be led through the task in such a way that they understand what they have to do, the sources they have been given to help them and the nature of the task they have been set. They should be given clear guidance about the amount of time to be spent on each section and the relative weighting of parts of the assignment.

   Whether the number of marks to be allocated to each sub-question should be shown is open to question. If sub-marks are given, this restricts the flexibility of levels mark schemes and of *post-hoc* marking. However, candidates do need to be made aware of the relative weighting of the questions.

5. The assignment itself must be clearly and simply expressed, so that candidates are in no doubt about the meaning of the question and what they are required to do. Complex sentence structures, double negatives, anything which will obscure the intention of the question should be avoided.

The language of sources: to adapt or not to adapt?

Both written and visual sources can cause problems. The issue of how far written sources should be adapted in the interests of accessibility is open to debate. Is it permissible to move away from the original source? Should difficult sources be rewritten or should glossaries be provided? If a suitable source cannot be found, why not invent appropriate sources in clear, straightforward language?

These are still contentious issues on which Chief Examiners themselves seem to differ and on which there would seem to be no common guidelines. The 1989 report of the Chief Examiners in History states 'Failure to adapt terminology and language could result in some sources being inaccessible to the less able. Over simplification could however mean that much of the value of the source was lost. Some examiners had no hesitation in changing abstract and technical terms. Others preferred to gloss technical terms' (SEAC, 1989).

It would seem that there is no common practice in this issue, but a number of useful points do emerge from the report.

- Given a range of sources from which to select, bear in mind the language difficulties of less able children.
- Abstract and technical language must be explained. What it the most effective way of doing this, through a glossary or by judicious rewriting or editing? I would suggest that the answer depends on the number of words and phrases which require explanation; a limited number can be glossaried but if you need to explain a good deal of the source, it can become very confusing to move continuously between the text and the glossary.
- Changing the source is a matter of degree. It is important to be clear on the purpose of the source. What is it there for? Why has it been included? If it is changed, will this detract from the purpose and therefore the value of the source? If the source is drastically altered, or indeed, altered at all, is this good history? What acknowledgement should be put on a source which has been substantially rewritten? Should students be told that the sources have been altered? (I would argue that the principles of 'good history' must be maintained and that if it is deemed necessary to change a source fundamentally, this must be acknowledged and explained.)

We should not be in the business of 'history made simple' but should do what we can to make a question accessible. We must however remember that we are attempting to devise assignments which enable the whole ability range to demonstrate what they know, understand and can do and that means having regard for the most able, as well as those students with learning difficulties. Moreover, having given access, we must then be able to differentiate and to assess genuine understanding and skills, not to delude the students and ourselves that they have achieved a higher level than is in fact the case. This only serves to make a mockery of assessment and to debase the study of history.

The Chief Examiners' Conference also gives a word of warning about visual sources, often regarded as simpler than written ones. Many teachers have discovered that visual sourses can also be problematic. Apart from the reprographic difficulties there is also the problem of the hidden messages and subtleties of many visual sources, in particular in the political cartoons beloved of the O-level papers.

At the end of the day, it may well not be possible to design an assignment in which all the sources are equally comprehensible across the ability range. Nor is this necessarily desirable, when it is the purpose of differentiation by outcome to assess the whole ability range. It is important that we present assignment in a format and language which is as clear and unambiguous as possible, and that we provide a ladder of access to historical questions which at first sight appear to be so challenging that they would seem to be denied to all but the most able. If we provide a structure which will help students work towards these 'big' questions, they may not all reach the top of the ladder but at least they are given the rungs to try!

Publications providing useful support and guidelines when considering this issue are included in the References section on p.65 (SEAC, 1989; SEC, 1988; Johnstone, 1988).

Structured questions

The use of structured questions is as much a teaching strategy as it is a means of assessment. It is for this reason that is figures so largely in the case study examples.

The use of structure can give access to a question, open it up and help pupils perceive links and connections they might not otherwise have made. Again, it can open up and clarify an issue which might otherwise seem obscure.

Structured questions can be used in a number of ways:

1. To help pupils appreciate a wider range of factors than might otherwise have occurred to them if they were simply presented with the 'big' question. Thus, the questions on the sources in the Prohibition case study were designed to act as a prompt to the range of attitudes towards Prohibition.

2. To help pupils find a logical route through a problem. This is of particular use when working towards a more open-ended question or extended narrative. Such structure helps with planning a coherent logical answer.

3. By using such structures often and overtly, pupils are helped to develop their own ideas of structure and to learn how to break down a seemingly daunting task into manageable steps.

4. As a teaching tool, issues or ideas which are too big to absorb in one gulp can be broken down into bite-size pieces and pupils are less likely to get lost on the way.

5. Tasks and assignments can be broken down into sub-questions which can, if necessary, build up to the final open-ended 'big' question which will be formally assessed. It is not necessary to mark all the sub-questions: they are designed to provide a ladder of access, not a longer assignment with more marking! On the other hand, the sub-questions can be an effective means of assessment, designed to elicit responses which do demonstrate understanding without the sheer size of the task seeming to be so daunting that it gets in the way.

Structured questions and stepped questions are not the same thing. They are designed to fulfil very different functions. In any mixed-ability group, there will be children operating at different level of ability. Stepped questions are directly related to these different ability levels. What is wrong with that? Nothing in so far as it goes, but it does not take long for experienced teachers to work out for themselves the hierarchy of ability within a class. All that stepped questions do is confirm that the teacher's perceptions are correct.

If that is the sole or prime function of assessment, stepped questions will do very well. However, assessment is concerned with much more than reinforcing what the teacher already knows about a child's performance. As John Fines says ' . . . the teacher's job is to *improve* the pupil's performance – assessment in only of real value if it is a teaching/learning situation in itself' (Fines, 1988).

The structured question therefore is designed to help the pupil understand what the whole question requires, to break down the task into a number of steps (hence, the frequent confusion with stepped questions) which will help the pupil to perceive the inner logic of the question which they can use to construct an answer, drawing from the structure and, in the process, appreciating the need to include points and arguments which may not be immediately apparent in the terse language of examination question.

The case studies which follow demonstrate how such a structure might be used in GCSE coursework assignments.

Case study: Structured questions

Assessment objective: Cause and consequence
Unit of work: The Russian Revolution, 1917
Topic: The causes of the 1917 Revolution

Pupils who are studying the Russian Revolution are bound to consider issues of causation: what where the long- and short-term causes of the Revolution? Why was Nicholas II forced to abdicate in February 1917? Why were the Bolsheviks successful in overthrowing the provisional government in October 1917? How far was the First World War a major factor in explaining the Revolutions of 1917?

The teaching, learning and assessment of pupils' understanding of causation do not have to be separate: pupils can acquire a structure as they learn about the Russian Revolution in such a way as to help them to understand why the Revolution took place and to provide a framework to help them to 'unpack' what at first sight looks like a daunting question through which their understanding is assessed.

The structure

1. *a) List the long-term causes for the abdication of the Tsar.*
   b) Lost the short-term causes for the abdication of the Tsar.
   c) List the long- and short-term causes in order of importance.
   Give reasons for your answer.
2. *Give two reasons why the provisional government was unpopular with the people of Russia.*
3. *What promises did Lenin make when he returned to Russia? Explain why these promises were popular with many people.*
4. *How did Trotsky prepare for the October Revolution?*
5. *Give three reasons why the Bolsheviks were able to overthrow the provisional government.*

Depending on how the activity is planned, these questions can be 'drip fed' to pupils as they are getting to grips with the events of the Revolution for the first time, or given as a recap once the teaching of the unit has been completed but before they embark on their assignment. In any event, students should be reminded of the structure questions when the assignment is given so that they can be encouraged to appreciate that these are key points to note when framing their responses.

There should be no mystery about the structure. Pupils should be encouraged to work together although they should each produce their own structure from which to work for the 'big' question which will be done as an individual assignment. The structure should be completed within a reasonable set time, leaving enough time for discussion of pupils' answers and and points to be raised.

Using this structure, pupils the embark on the question itself, having been pointed in the direction of issues which should be considered by the discussion of the structure. The circumstances in which the assignment is completed will depend on the rationale for setting the assignment. If a prime consideration is to give practice at working to a strict time-limit under examination conditions, the assignment should be completed to time, in class, working in silence. Nor should such experience be denied. All GCSE history courses demand examination answers and examination conditions can be off-putting if candidates are not used to the discipline of the examination hall. If, however, such practice is not the main criterion, there can be greater flexibility and pupils should be given the chance to complete the assignment for homework. The dangers of collaboration or unfair parental assistance are outweighed by the opportunity to move beyond the constraints of the examination, especially if sixty to seventy per cent (depending on the examination group) is assessed through the examination. If the assignment arises naturally out of classroom work and is started in class and if all pupils have access to the same sources, those pupils who need extra time and are prepared to put in extra private work outside the classroom should be given the opportunity to show what they know, understand and can do.

The use of structured questions as a regular part of classroom practice makes pupils aware of the structure behind the essay, so that, by the time they take GCSE, many of them should be able to create their own structures to help them to unpack seemingly complex questions. The ability to break down a complex task is also an invaluable asset to transfer to A-level history where it provides help in planning and constructing the analytical arguments demanded in the conventional A-level essay (see p. 61)

The assignment question

When the Tsar was forced to abdicate in February, 1917, was there bound to be a second Revolution in October, 1917?

ASSIGNMENT MARK SCHEME

OBJECTIVE TARGET: CAUSATION
Level 1
Partial narrative, which gives some explanation of why the Tsar abdicated and the Bolsheviks took control but does not make causal link explicit.

Level 2
Traces causal link which suggests one or two causes for the abdication of the Tsar and the overthrow of the provisional government. Does not make connections between the causes.

Level 3
Suggests a number of causes for the overthrow of the Tsar and the provisional government and makes connections between the causes (causal web).

Level 4
Makes judgments about the relative importance of the causes to explain the overthrow of the Tsar and the provisional government.

Comment

An issue raised by this assignment is the place of the essay in GCSE. How important is the ability to express ideas as a coherent narrative? The expectation seems to be that pupils who are achieving the higher levels should be expressing their responses in such a way, but it must be clear that the ability to develop a coherent, sustained argument was not the target objective for the assignment. On the other hand, it is hard to see how the highest levels can be achieved if the pupil does not have the ability to marshal his or her knowledge and understanding in a logical, ordered fashion.

With the demands of A level in mind, it is no bad thing if at least one GCSE coursework assignment does require more extended writing, but the target objective to be assessed must be clear. Of course, fluency of expression and the ability to organise and plan resources often go hand in hand with higher levels of understanding but not always: pupils can demonstrate a high level of understanding of causation when their ability to produce an elegantly constructed essay is more limited. Assessing the evidence of understanding and distinguishing this from the ability to construct a coherent argument needs care.

Gifted pupils and high attainers need opportunities to show what they can know, understand and can do as well as those with learning difficulties. Questions and the structure of the assignment should not be so tight that the more able pupils are denied more challenging work.

Case study: The interrogation and evaluation of sources

Assessment objective: The evaluation of historical sources
Unit of work: Changing attitudes towards poverty and the founding of the Welfare State.

In some ways GCSE assessment objective 3.3, 'the evaluation of historical sources', is considered by many teachers to be the most familiar and to pose the least problems in terms of devising coursework assignments. Increasingly, source-based work has become both familiar and integrated within history teaching. Pupils are constantly encouraged to work from a variety of sources, whatever the assessment objective.

We should therefore be encouraging pupils to interrogate and evaluate sources all the time, but, precisely because of this, isolating source evaluation for assessment purposes, can cause difficulties. After all, asking questions of and about the sources should be fundamental to the study of history as a whole and to separate-out source evaluation as a particular assessment objective can distort the study of history.

The following exercise is made up of a series of questions which could be given to pupils to consider whilst they are studying changing attitudes towards the poor in late nineteenth-century Britain and the founding of the Welfare State. Designed to help pupils to develop an understanding of the source and of the ideas contained within them, questions 1–5 are intended to provide the structure for the task and not to be part of the formal GCSE assessment.

The assignment is focused on question 6 for which a suggested levels-of-response mark scheme is provided. It is this question which targets objective 3.3, 'source evaluation'. Responses will provide evidence of attainment against this assessment objective. The other questions are designed to develop skills of source evaluation but will also help pupils develop their understanding of the topic as a whole.

> Few of the 200 families who lived there occupied more than one room. In little rooms, no more than eight feet square, would be found living father, mother and several children. Fifteen rooms out of twenty were filthy to the last degree.

Not a room would be free from vermin. The little yard at the back was only sufficient for dustbin and closet and water-tap, serving for six or seven families. The water would be drawn from cisterns which were receptacles for refuse and perhaps occasionally a dead cat.

[A] A description of Shelton Street from *The Life and Labour of People in London* by Charles Booth, 1902–3

Charles Booth produced one of the first detailed surveys of living conditions in the poorer areas of London, based on several years work of detailed observation.

First, the information given does not refer to selected cases. Secondly there has been absolutely no exaggeration. This must be to every Christian heart a loud and bitter cry, appealing for the help which it is the supreme mission of the Church to supply.

You have to penetrate courts reeking with poisonous and malodorous gases arising from the accumulation of sewage and refuse scattered in all directions: courts, many of them which the sun never penetrates, which are never visited by a breath of fresh air. You have to ascend rotten staircases. You have to grope your way along dark and filthy passages swarming with vermin, then you may gain admittance to the dens in which these thousands of being who belong as much as you to the race for whom Christ died, herd together.

[B] From *The Bitter Cry of the Outcast London* by the Rev Andrew Mearns, 1883

Reverend Mearns was one of a number of clergymen who wrote about the slums of the industrial cities, believing that it was the duty of the Church to bring such conditions to the attention of all Christians.

The life of a labourer is marked by five alternating periods of want and comparative plenty. During early childhood, unless his father is a skilled worker, he will probably be in poverty; this will last until he or some of his brothers or sisters begin to earn money and thus augment their father's wages sufficiently to raise the family above the poverty line. Then follows the period during which he is earning money and living under his parents' roof: for some portion of this period he will be earning more money than is required for lodging, food and clothes. This is his chance to save money. If he had saved enough money for furnishing a cottage, this period of prosperity may continue after marriage until he has two or three children, when poverty will again overtake him. This period of poverty will last perhaps ten years, i.e. until the first child is fourteen years old and beings to earn wages, but if there are more than three children it may last longer. While the children are earning and before they leave home to marry the man enjoys another period of prosperity – possibly however only to sink back into poverty when his children have married and left him and he himself is too old for work, for his income has never permitted him saving enough for him and his wife to live upon for more than a short time.

[C] From *Poverty: A Study of Town Life* by Seebohn Rowntree, 1901

Rowntree produced a detailed study of the poorer areas of York at the end of the nineteenth century. Rowntree himself came from the wealthy family which was one of the main employers in York. The evidence produced by Rowntree and Booth had a great impact on the Liberal Government which was elected in 1906 and which started the Welfare State.

Help from without is often enfeebling [weakening] in its effects, but help from within invariably invigorates [makes stronger]. Whatever is done for men or classes, to a certain extent takes away the stimulus and necessity of doing for themselves; and where men are subjected to over-guidance and over government, the inevitable tendency is to render them comparatively helpless.

[D] From *Self Help* by Samuel Smiles, 1859

Samuel Smiles was a great believer in '*laissez faire*' and was opposed to what he believed was government interference in people's lives. He believed that people should be free to make what they could of their lives.

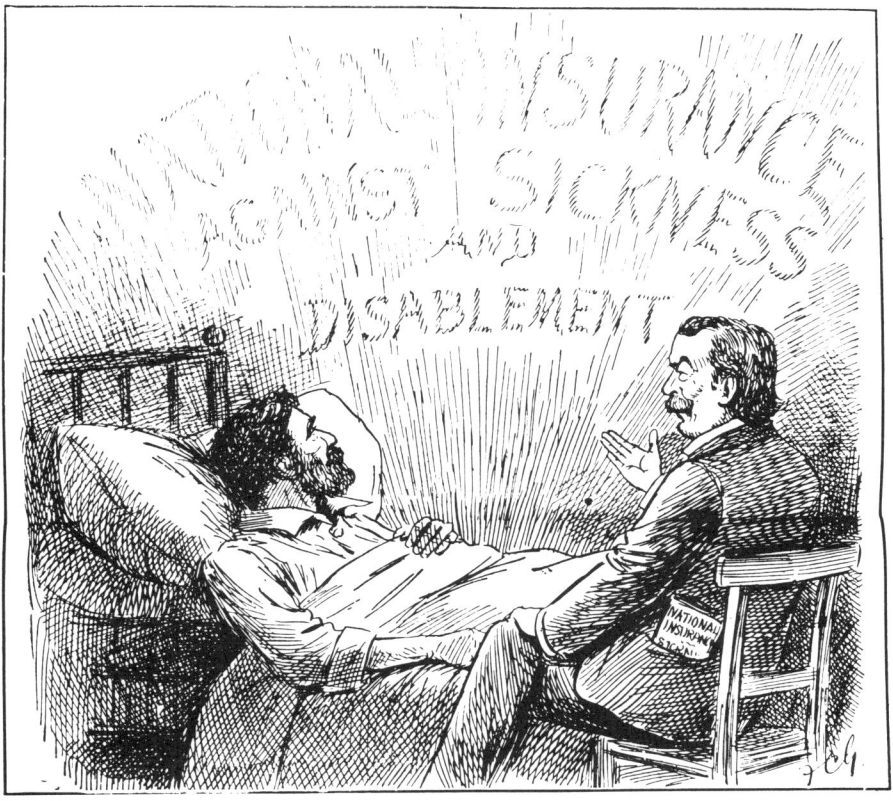

[E] From *Punch* on the introduction of the National Insurance Bill, 1911

[F] From *Punch* on the introduction of the Pensions Act, 1908

The following questions can be 'drip fed' to pupils for consideration whilst they are studying the topic. The whole exercise can then be given to pupils so that they can be reminded of the issues they have already considered in preparation for the final question in which they will be assessed.

1. *Look at sources A and B. Identify three points made in both sources about the living conditions of the poor.*

2. *Why does the author of source B believe that something should be done about the conditions he describes?*

3. *Should source C be regarded as an accurate factual account of what life was like in York in the late nineteenth century? Give reasons for your answer.*

4. *Which people do you think would support the arguments put forward in source D. Explain your answer.*

5. *Explain how cartoons E and F give different opinions about Lloyd George. Why do you think people had different opinions about him?*

6. The assessment question

Look carefully at sources A to F

Draw up a chart under the headings listed below:

Source no.	Author	What questions does source answer?	Value

On the chart write the source number, who wrote/produced it, what it tells you about attitudes to the poor and the conditions they lived in and what value you think the source is to a historian who is writing about the beginning of the Welfare State.

Use the chart to answer the following questions in as much detail as you can:

> *Which if these sources do you think is of the greatest value to a historian of this period? Use the sources to explain your answer fully.*

MARK SCHEME
Target Objective: Evaluation of evidence (Provenance and value of sources).

(Note: This mark scheme refers to question 6 only.)

Level 1
Judges worth on the basis of volume of information without judging the value of that information.

Level 2
Recognises that volume of information is not enough. Recognises the need to assess objectivity of the author.

Level 3
Recognises that authors have differing perspectives and will give different points of view.

Level 4
Recognises that sources can be written for different audiences

Level 5
Recognises that the value of the source depends on the nature of the enquiry and the questions asked.

Differentiation by outcome: the use of levels of response

Differentiation by outcome entails setting a common task for the full ability range and assessing the candidates' positive achievements by assessing their response to the task against a levels-of-response mark scheme, devised in draft form in advance of reading the responses and amended in the light of those responses. Such mark schemes should be designed so that clear progression can be seen between the levels and (if this is considered necessary or desirable) mark bands are allocated to each level to discriminate between responses within a particular level.

For many teachers, this approach to assessment was one of the most challenging aspects of GCSE. Many mark schemes, including many of the exemplars provided by the examination groups, did not demonstrate progression in conceptual understanding but rather a 'little, more, most' incremental increase which was based more on historical information than on historical understanding.

Teachers were told that assessment must arise naturally out of the course, yet for many differentiation by outcome meant marking everything twice and spending hours on moderating; levels-of-response mark schemes were time consuming and tentative because they were little understood and therefore produced only for those assignments to be submitted as GCSE coursework. Thus for many the level-of-response mark scheme has come to take on a mystique which has yet to be penetrated, and some teachers freely admit that they still approach them with diffidence!

The fact that those teachers who had experience of the Schools History Project tended to be more confident in handling levels-of-response mark schemes should surely serve to demonstrate that with practice, it is possible for such an approach to assessment, as a fundamental part of teaching, to be integrated much more into normal classroom practice. Marking homework, giving a grade, a comment at the end, all involve assessment. Similarly, when we write a report, respond to a query from a colleague about a particular pupil, talk to parents on parents' evening, we are making assessments. Time was, when we were required for CSE to estimate grades for the candidates in advance of the examination. We were not often wildly wrong in our assessments. Why then, for some, the concern about levels-of-response marking and what it entails?

A levels-of-response approach formalises much of what we have always done, but in doing so it obliges us to become more precise and less woolly in our perceptions of pupil performance. An 'impression' mark is usually roughly right but can we be confident that we have diagnosed the specific strengths and weaknesses of a pupil's understanding unless the assignment is targeted on specific objectives and unless we have thought through what we perceive to be progression in that objective? In fact can we make valid judgments about a pupil's progress which can be both formative (and thus give advice on how performance might be improved) and summative (and give a fully accurate objective assessment on what the pupil has achieved) unless we ourselves are absolutely clear what it is we are assessing and have some criteria against which to assess?

Again, GCSE experience provides the basis on which to draw in order to meet National Curriculum requirements. Teacher assessment entails monitoring pupil progress against specific assessment objectives. National Curriculum history may provide programmes of study and statements of attainment but we will have the professional responsibility for devising schemes of work and assignments through which we can accurately assess pupil performance using the statements of attainment.

National Curriculum assessment will seem less challenging if we build on the experience of GCSE and attempt to integrate levels-of-response marking much more into our normal classroom practice. Apart from anything else, the more familiar the approach, the easier it is to operate.

There should be no mystery about levels, either to pupils or to teachers. Pupils should be made aware of the levels concept long before they embark on their GCSE course. They should understand that here is a ladder of access which should be explained: this is what you have to do if you want to climb the ladder. It is not an obstacle race but a means of positive assessment to show what the pupil knows, understands and can do.

The mark schemes provided in the case studies are not intended to be the perfect solution. Many colleagues may well disagree with the level statements, which in many ways is as it should be. Such general-purpose mark schemes which were produced in many of the books which flooded the market in the initial response to GCSE were very misleading. Levels mark schemes are best produced at the same time as the assignment is devised so that the assessment objective on which the assignment is focuses is reflected in the mark scheme.

Links between GCSE assessment and the National Curriculum

I have already stated my concern about the perception that we have 'done' GCSE and that further INSET and development work is not necessary. This perception by many teachers and LEAs has largely come about because of the advent of the National Curriculum. In 1986, GCSE was for many teachers the biggest single centrally imposed curriculum change of their career.

Since then, the goal posts have moved considerably. GCSE pales into insignificance against the impact of the National Curriculum – hence the understandable feeling that concerns about GCSE have been overtaken. However, that would be to ignore the real link between GCSE and the way forward within the National Curriculum which reflects many of the lessons learned from GCSE. Strategies being developed to respond to the demands of GCSE will be of considerable benefit in the future.

It is now clear that GCSE will be the main form of assessment for many at the end of Key Stage 4, and that Key Stage 4 history will be assessed either as a single subject GCSE in its own right (Model 2, final Order) or in combination with geography or other subjects (Model 1, final Order). SEAC has already published proposals for the cross-referencing of GCSE grades to National Curriculum levels of attainment. It is proposed that GCSE grades should be awarded to pupils who have achieved National Curriculum levels 4–10. National Curriculum levels 1–3 will not be assessed at GCSE.

It is also clear that much of the GCSE assessment model has survived into the National Curriculum. The attainment targets assess understanding of change and continuity over time, of causation, of the evaluation of historical evidence, and, there are even strong hints of similarity and difference and empathy embedded in AT1, all of which can be found in the GCSE national criteria for assessment.

What of levels of response and differentiation by outcome? Initial work with the statements of attainment would suggest that, once again, it is a question of building on what has been learned through GCSE. Certainly, assessment of attainment in the National Curriculum is pointing in the same direction as GCSE and experience and expertise gained over the last four years will stand us in very good stead as we endeavour to get to grips with what is to come!

For those teachers who follow a modern world syllabus, there is much which is familiar in the proposed programmes of study for Key Stage 4. However, all teachers, whatever the content area of the syllabus they are currently following will need to look beyond the content *per se* to the assessment model laid down in the National Curriculum final Orders. This is the key factor which enshrines much of the thinking of the Schools History Project which in turn underpins the GCSE National Criteria.

Those cluster groups which brought together schools in the same examining group in the area and which in some cases began to work to develop common coursework assignment could well become the embryo support groups which will be vital for the support and self-help which will be essential to meet the demands of the National Curriculum.

2
Assessment in the junior secondary years

The lessons of GCSE

The implications of GCSE for teaching and learning in the junior secondary years became clear as soon as we embarked on GCSE. Obviously, pupils would respond more positively to the GCSE National Criteria if they were familiar with the concepts and skills which are assessed by those criteria before embarking on the GCSE course. The introduction of GCSE therefore had implications for the schemes of work, for process and for assessment.

To an extent, assessment in the junior secondary years has always been influenced, if not dominated by the assessment requirements of 16+. When multiple choice was affirmed in GCE/CSE examinations, it became a common form of testing in the junior secondary years. If at sixteen candidates were required to write a number of largely narrative accounts against the clock, so should they in years 1 to 3 (Y7–9). If candidates were given sources as stimulus and for comprehension, this too was introduced lower down the school. If the emphasis in GCE and CSE was on recall, so it should be in lower school examinations.

Assessment in GCSE history has raised issues which challenge some of the assumptions which seem to have underpinned junior secondary assessment procedures for many years.

The need for a clearly defined policy on assessment, both whole-school and within a history department has been further underlined in the past two years by the developments in profiling and records of achievement and by the introduction and implementation of the National Curriculum.

Once again, I would argue that the starting point in the secondary school should be the lessons we have learned and are learning from GCSE. Discussion about targeted objectives, about differentiation and levels-of-response mark schemes applies equally to assessment in the junior secondary years. If pupils are familiar with assessment tasks which focus on National Criteria objectives by the time they embark on the GCSE course in Year 10, if they have tackled source evaluation exercises and have considered cause and consequence, similarity and difference, continuity and change, the role of an individual, and have practised deploying their knowledge to build-up a coherent, logical response, the demands of GCSE will seem far less daunting. Indeed, even before GCSE, the traditional approach to assessment in the junior secondary years had been challenged, in particular by the introduction of modular approaches where assessment was an integral part of the module, thus questioning the need for an end-of-year examination.

The role and function of homework in relation to assessment also needs to be considered. Often perceived as an extension of classroom activity (as indeed it should be) homework is marked or graded by the teacher but is seen as distinct from the tests and examinations. Tasks set for homework and assessed by the teacher on the contrary must be seen as an integral part of the assessment system. Homework assignments therefore must be targeted on defined assessment objectives as much as any other form of assessment.

Furthermore, we must start to work towards a coherent marking system which integrates all forms of assessment in a manner which is clear and which has been explained to both pupils and their parents. At present it is not unusual for pupils to be on the receiving end of grades: A–E, marks out of ten or twenty, comments – sometimes helpful, sometimes anodyne – ticks and crosses, levels statements, profile and records of achievement levels. Faced with this plethora of reporting assessment outcomes, small wonder the pupil is confused. If the integration of assessment procedures is to mean anything, a clear, common marking system must be applied so that pupils fully understand, not only the objectives on which the assessment is based, but also the criteria by which they have been assessed and how those criteria relate to the mark they have been given. The National Curriculum provides the ideal opportunity to bring some coherence to our marking systems and to devise a school-based marking policy which integrates National Curriculum attainment with records of achievement in a way which is helpful and meaningful for both pupil and parent.

National Curriculum history also brings progression into sharper focus. Unlike GCSE, there is little published research into progression at junior secondary level. Suggested levels mark schemes must therefore be regarded as provisional and subject to revision based on trial and error. The same must be true of the National Curriculum statements of attainment. Indeed there are already signs that the publication of the final Orders have led to a number of research proposals which, in future years may lead to changes in the statements of attainment, although one may hope for a period of stability. However, we have to acknowledge that, for the first time, we have a coherent framework for teaching history to five to sixteen-year-olds and, for the first time we are in a position to observe a coherent pattern of progression.

Just as with GCSE, teachers will come to interpret the reality of the statements of attainment when they are in a position to make observations based on pupils' work which they can then relate to the statements. This is not in any way to deny the basic philosophy that assessment must be for defined purposes, whether diagnostic, formative or summative, that the assessment objectives must be clear and defined and that the tasks must be appropriate and allow pupils to show positive achievement.

I intend to focus on three key areas where assessment in the junior secondary years is concerned: links with GCSE, profiling and records of achievement and the implications of the National Curriculum.

Assessment and progression

By focusing as teachers on defined criteria in GCSE and the National Curriculum, we too become familiar with targeting assignments towards specific objectives, with differentiation by outcome and with levels-of-response marking.

This is not to pretend that the move towards targeted objectives and defined assessment criteria is easy. Old habit die hard and we need to be convinced that change is necessary. This is why we should question the purpose of assessment. Why is it necessary to have assessment criteria and levels-of-response mark schemes? One answer has already been given, namely the need to prepare for the demands of GCSE. If that is what is required at sixteen, clearly children and teachers need to work towards this goal in a planned coherent fashion so that, at sixteen, the pupil can be helped to achieve the grade of which he/she is capable. There are wider considerations. However much the criteria themselves may be debated and disputed, in general it is affirmed that the move towards defined, conceptual criteria has meant a move away from meaningless rote learning. This shift of emphasis has been affirmed by the TGAT Report: children demonstrate their knowledge when they show that they can use what they know. Thus, if assessment is focused on the *use* of knowledge to show how far children understand and are able to use what they know, and if that assessment arises naturally out of what normally takes place in the classroom, it follows that the whole teaching and learning experience should be focusing on encouraging understanding by active learning and assessing that understanding in a way that can measure progression. This approach underpins the National Curriculum proposals and the relationship between the study units in the programmes of study and the attainment targets.

This is where the levels come in. As I have already stated, no one would assume that the current state of research about progression in history is the final word. Nonetheless, however imperfect our current thinking may be, devising levels mark schemes is a most effective way to concentrate the mind on progression. Nor should it be a case of accepting someone else's perceptions of levels without question. The continuing experience of devising and refining levels mark schemes is by far the most effective way of turning general observations about progression into more specific and exact statements of how a child is developing. Based on those statements, one can make far more specific and helpful comments to parents and pupils.

Preparation for GCSE in the lower secondary years therefore should entail assessment assignments which are specifically targeted on particular objectives, an approach which has now been enshrined in the National Curriculum Orders in which the attainment targets define the objectives, the statements of attainment attempt to chart general progression within these objectives and the study units in the programmes of study provide the historical context within which, through which and for which this understanding is to be developed. The relationship between the study units and attainment targets is explained fully in *Non-statutory Guidance* from the NCC, which gives a great deal of helpful and supportive advice about putting theory into practice (NCC, April 1991).

Towards the National Curriculum

From September 1991, National Curriculum history became part of the school curriculum for Key Stages 1, 2, and 3 and from September 1994, will be so for Key Stage 4. SATs for Key Stage 3 will be administered for the first time (unrecorded) in 1994. Key Stage 4 (GCSE) will make its first appearance in 1986. After some debate, it now seems likely that SEAC will not change the subject-specific national criteria for GCSE before 1995. Therefore, there will be a further four years of GCSE history which must conform to the present National Criteria.

We are continuing to move towards criterion-referenced assessment, in which the assessment objectives (attainment targets) are conceptual or methodological. Pupil performance will therefore be assessed against statements of attainment which themselves demonstrate progression in understanding of chronology, causation and change (AT1), interpretations (AT2), and the use and analysis of historical evidence (AT3).

The assessment of historical knowledge

Where does this approach leave the content of history? Is it the intention to deny the importance of historical knowledge because it will not be assessed?

Exactly what is meant by historical knowledge needs further consideration. Too often 'knowledge' has been used as a synonym for content or information. Children demonstrate their knowledge by using historical information effectively, and they use that information effectively when they use it to demonstrate an increasingly sophisticated understanding of the concepts and methodology which form the basis of the attainment targets. Historical knowledge is not assessable through mindless factual recall which might demonstrate a good memory or a possible potential as a contestant in *Mastermind* but it achieves little else. Therefore, in order to demonstrate what they know, understand and can do (again the link with GCSE), historical information must be assessed in context and that context must enable the pupil to progress conceptually and methodologically.

This is not to deny the importance of the information base. Indeed, it is crucial. Concepts and skills cannot be assessed in a vacuum; indeed there should be an expectation that as pupils advance up the levels ladder, so their stock of historical information on which they can draw in order to illustrate, demonstrate and make connections will increase. Their historical knowledge will deepen as they apply an increasingly sophisticated understanding of the concepts and skills fundamental to the study of history to a larger information base. Thus they will have more 'knowledge' at their disposal to support the attainment targets, to make connections and to draw conclusions.

Most advocates of the Schools History Project would accept this argument. What may seem more unpalatable is the perceived need to give some direction, indeed prescription, to what that information base should be. This is where we enter the minefield of selection and prescription of content, with the perception that, by definition, selection must lead to political statements of 'whose history?' and to social engineering of the purpose of school history.

What are the implications of this debate for the assessment of National Curriculum history?

1. Because 'historical facts' have not been singled out for assessment this means that a body of information has not been selected as having particular significance through being selected for assessment. The concepts and methodological attainment targets can and should be applied to all the content areas taught.

2. The existence of Attainment Target 2 is of key significance in avoiding the promotion of a particular line and the expectation that there is one correct interpretation. The integration of AT2 in the planning of history schemes of work should enable pupils to come to realise and understand that historical evidence is partial, reasons why it is partial and that such evidence is open to interpretations which can be and are challenged for a number of reasons. In short, AT2 ensures that the study of history enable pupils to *know with doubt*.

3. The information base of National Curriculum history is undoubtedly more defined than has previously been the case. The Final Report of the History Working Group (DES, 1990) explains that choices have been made and gives the Group's criteria for making those choices. Pupils will be assessed through the attainment targets, but that assessment must be based on the content defined in the study units in the programmes of study, which also have statutory enforcement.

4. National Curriculum assessment will therefore be based on conceptual and methodological attainment targets which overlay the information base of the study units in the programmes of study. Schemes of work must therefore be devised in which the programmes of study are taught in such a way that the attainment targets can be assessed. In the final Orders this relationship which is at the heart of National Curriculum history is further explained and developed in the general requirements for the programmes of study which demonstrate the variety of ways in which this link can and should be made. Further support is given in *Non-statutory Guidance*.

Teacher assessment

Because of the relationship between programmes of study and attainment targets and because certain study units (information bases) have been allocated to particular key stages, the proposed relationship between teacher assessment and SATs in National Curriculum history is particularly important. Indeed, far from marginalising the teacher's role in the assessment process, school-based pupil assessment, record keeping and reporting will be central.

SATs will be administered towards the end of each key stage. In between times, teachers will be required to record pupil performance and to report to parents once a year. Parents also have the right to request evidence of their child's National Curriculum attainment which schools must produce within fifteen days. Thus teachers will need to be able to monitor pupil performance in the attainment targets year by year and to keep examples of pupils' work as evidence of that attainment.

Does this mean that the entire curriculum is going to be assessment-dominated? Will teachers be going round carrying check-boards, looking for any evidence that a particular level has been reached so that they can put a tick in a box? Certainly these fears have been expressed, and they are very justifiable fears, if assessment is seen as a bolt-on extra and not as an integral part of the teaching and learning process.

Here, the argument comes full circle. Assessment has been and always will be an integral and central part of teaching. As teachers, we make informal and formal judgments about our pupils all the time. The purpose of GCSE, profiling and records of achievement and now the National Curriculum is to make that assessment process more objective and systematic but it remains an integral part of the process.

Chapter 8 of the Final Report of the History Working Group emphasised that both teacher assessment and SATs should derive from the same principles, namely:

- to encourage and support good classroom practice;
- to foster the development of good assessment practice – in particular to ensure that assessment results are as fair and reliable as possible;

- to ensure that assessment demands on teachers and pupils are practical in terms of time;
- to ensure that assessment fits naturally and easily into the curriculum.

How are these principles to be ensured? If the good practice of GCSE and the profiling movement have been taken on board, they are well on the way to being achieved. In particular, methods of assessment must be reviewed to ensure that they do fit naturally and easily into normal classroom practice. If not, National Curriculum assessment will become the burden feared by so many – and it need not and should not be so.

Possible strategies which can avoid such assessment domination might be:

- The use of assessment objectives as an integral part of the planning process. The attainment targets which define these assessment objectives also provide possible routes through the content of the study units. Thus the attainment targets should be regarded as defining the teaching and learning objectives as well as the assessment objectives. The use of key questions in the planning of schemes of work is an effective way of bringing the content, skills and processes together.

- The design of classroom activities which provide appropriate opportunities for gathering evidence for assessment as well as for helping pupils to develop their understanding and knowledge. Activities for teaching and learning and assessment tasks should not be regarded as separate and mutually exclusive. The same activity, if designed to focus on an attainment target and a range of levels within that attainment target can fulfil both functions simultaneously.

- The range of methods of assessment. Pupils do not have to be assessed through written exercises under test conditions, although such an approach is valid, especially if the teacher wishes to ensure that the pupils' work is unaided and produced under the same conditions. However recall itself is not an assessment objective and the assessment task should not depend on it.

- GCSE and profiling have been based on differentiation by outcome. Will this approach continue? Devising assessment tasks appropriate for the whole ability range has its difficulties; we should be moving towards the use of a range of differentiation strategies; not just by outcome, but also, on occasions, by task, and certainly involving a range of appropriate resources and teaching strategies.

Methods of assessment should embrace much more than individual written exercises, and should encompass oral and group work, drama, IT, and a whole range of written tasks.

It is much more important that the attainment targets are revisited frequently throughout the year, rather than one large assessment exercise to assess each attainment be set at the end of each history study unit. It has already been noted that progression in history is not linear. To achieve consistency and reliability pupils must be given the opportunity to revisit the assessment objective on a number of occasions, using a range of different contexts, i.e. in a variety of study units. Indeed teacher assessment can be based on a number of small, contained tasks, started in a lesson and completed for a single homework.

This of course has implications for record-keeping. To record grades or marks for homework assignments is common practice. If one has started to think about specific assessment objectives for GCSE and profiling, it is not a large step to integrate regular homework and the records of grades into this system.

Division of the record book for the year into the three attainment targets and the strands in AT1 enable levels to be recorded depending on pupil performance against the statements of attainment as assignments are completed. When reporting to parents, the level achieved in a particular attainment target for a number of assignments is immediately apparent. Some consistency will allow the teacher to make a judgment about a level of attainment.

Although all programmes of study should be capable of delivering all the attainment targets, nonetheless, it is possible that teachers may wish to use their professional judgment to give a particular focus to the work being studied. Thus, it is not necessary to juggle the three attainment targets to the same extent all the time, as long as in the course of the year, sufficient evidence has been collected to enable the teacher to report pupil progress to parents.

In the same way, not all the content defined in the study units needs to be assessed. As *Non-statutory Guidance* makes very clear, it is for the teacher to decide, with the aid of the FOCUS statement at the top of each core study unit, which areas of content should be the basis for depth studies and which will provide the context, framework and outline for the study (NCC, 1991). As far as the supplementary study units are concerned, it is left to the teacher to decide the main focus of the study for him/herself. It is likely that assessment tasks will derive mainly from the areas to be studies in depth and will be based on the key questions which the teacher has decided should be the focus of the study

Standard assessment tests (standard national tests)

The emphasis has undoubtedly switched recently from task to test – and to short, written tests at that. The specification for the Key Stage 3 test in history indicates that the end of Key Stage 3 test will take the form of two, one-hour written tests, to be taken under controlled conditions by all Year 9 pupils on dates specified by SEAC, externally set and marked by teachers to mark schemes devised by the SAT developers. The SAT will be based on two or three core study units, with the possibility of general questions covering the whole of the programme of study.

It must however be remembered that it is the pupil's understanding as defined by the statements of attainment in the attainment targets that is being tested. As with teacher assessment, the attainment targets must be applied to the content of the study units and the SAT developers will need to ensure that this is in fact achieved.

It is to be hoped that the History Working Group's affirmation of the close relationship between teacher assessment and the SAT is recognised so that, as with records of achievement, the formative informs the summative and both are based on sound assessment principles and practice.

Progression in the attainment targets

The statements of attainment chart the progress in a pupil's historical understanding. However, such progression has its dangers (as pointed out in the Final Report). To define conceptual and methodological progression in TGAT terms of ten discrete levels is, to say the least, challenging. There are those who claim that this cannot and will not work in history.

The statements do obviously represent progression, but one must be aware that much of this territory is largely uncharted, As yet, there is relatively little research into how children learn history, particularly in the lower secondary years. Furthermore, that research which has been generated by GCSE has led teachers to extrapolate downwards when devising profiling statements. For the first time an attempt has been made to establish progression from Level 1 to Level 10, 5–16. It may be that in the light of practical classroom experience, these statements will need revising. It is already the case that this exercise is encouraging further research based on objective evidence into how children learn history.

It is also possible that the statements of attainment which apply to children as they enter the lower secondary years (average Level 4) will seem very challenging in comparison with current expectations, but for the first time in the teaching of school history, pupils will be building up their conceptual and methodological understanding systematically from the age of five. Therefore, by eleven, many children should have achieved considerable mastery of the skills and concepts involved. That, at least is the theory; it must be recognised that the INSET and resource implications to put theory into practice are enormous.

Case study: The statements of attainment and levels-of-response mark schemes

In the debate which has surrounded the introduction of National Curriculum history, many concerns have been expressed about the TGAT ten-level model and how far this can be made applicable to history. Many teachers with the GCSE experience of levels-of-response mark schemes behind them were puzzled by the proposed statements of attainment produced by the History Working Group because they seemed to be very general and were by no means always hierarchical as descriptors of progression. How could these statements be used as a levels mark scheme?

The amendments produced by NCC and the statements as they have now appeared in the final Orders are to an extent more straightforward but the linear progression is still lacking. True, there are groups of statements which can be taken together, but there are other occasions when the levels statements empathetically do not represent a hierarchical 'run'. For example, AT1 L6b) requires pupils to recognise that causes and consequences can vary in importance, whereas L3–5 have focused on the understanding of the multi-causal nature of history.

It is unlikely that a pupil will show an understanding of the degrees of importance in a question which is attempting to elicit a response about types of causes. Equally, the hierarchical relationship between AT1c) L5 'show how different features in a historical situation relate to each other' and AT1c) L6 'describe the different ideas and attitudes of people in a historical situation' seems somewhat remote!

The point is that the statements of attainment are not and were never intended to be a glorified ten-levels mark scheme. They are general descriptions about a pupil's progress and must be related by the teacher to a specific context. This might be done through a levels mark scheme or, more loosely by relating the task to the statements.

In some cases, as demonstrated below, it is possible to link a 'run' of statements of attainment to a particular task. In other cases, it might be necessary to 'unpack' a particular statement of attainment.

It is very important to remember that the statements are general descriptors and that a pupil will not automatically move from one level to the next within a short space of time. Indeed, the original TGAT model predicated a move through a level roughly every two years.

For diagnostic purposes, it is also necessary at times to unpack the statements and to make them accessible to pupils by devising smaller steps within the statement.

The teacher uses his/her professional judgment to decide what evidence is necessary to demonstrate that a particular National Curriculum level has been achieved. It is likely in the course of a year that a combination of the approaches outlined above will be used. At times, the task will be designed to focus on a particular level, at others, a range of levels will be accessed through a task-specific levels-of-response mark scheme. There may well be occasions when a particular levels statement is unpacked, also using a task-specific mark scheme.

The following example below shows how a levels-of-response mark scheme can be related to the National Curriculum levels:

Question 1

1. What were medieval kings meant to do?

MARK SCHEME: QUESTION 1

Level 1
A simple description of (a) function(s) with little support from the sources.

Level 2
A description of function(s) which is supported by evidence from the sources.

Level 3
A description of one or more functions, well supported by the sources sufficient to show a process of deduction about the power and authority of the king from the sources.

Level 4
As Level 3 but showing awareness of the wide range of functions and duties.

Level 5
Uses evidence from a synthesis of sources to support deductions.

Level 6
A coherent description, drawn from a range of sources of the role and functions of a medieval king.

Question 2

2. How did medieval kings make themselves special?
   Why would they want to be seen as special?
   Why did people accept the rule of the king?

MARK SCHEME: QUESTION 2
Level 1
Answer which refers to physical power: 'because he had an army'.

Level 2
Answer which refers to his office or position and explains that the authority of the king was accepted as a matter of law and belief.

Level 3
As Level 2, but explains the origins of the authority in terms of religion, supernatural power.

For those pupils who had achieved the higher levels in this question, an extension question was also prepared

Extension question

What do these beliefs tell us about life in medieval times?

MARK SCHEME: EXTENSION QUESTION
Level 1
Describes rather than explains beliefs and their links with medieval life and circumstances.

Level 2
Answer which shows how a circumstance in medieval life might foster a belief, e.g. belief in supernatural cures shows lacks of medical knowledge/ability to cure disease naturally.

Level 3
As Level 2, but addresses a range of beliefs and aspects of life and recognises different value systems and sets of beliefs and the reasons for this.

LEVELS OF RESPONSE: QUESTION 1
Level 1
Below base line: NC level not achieved.

Level 2
AT3 L2: Recognise that historical sources can stimulate and help answer questions about the past.

Level 3
AT3 L3: Make deductions from historical sources.

Level 4
AT3 L3: Make deductions from historical sources.

Level 5
AT3 L4: Put together information drawn from different historical sources.

Level 6
AT3 L4

LEVELS OF RESPONSE: QUESTION 2
Level 1
No evidence of attainment at AT1c).

Level 2
AT1c): Possible evidence of L6 'describe different ideas and attitudes of people in a historical situation'.

Level 3
AT1c): Clear evidence of L6.

LEVELS OF RESPONSE: EXTENSION QUESTION
Level 3
Response required for clear evidence of AT1c) L7.

At the end of the day, it is the teacher's professional duty to provide the evidence of attainment. From what we know about progression in understanding in history, pupils must be offered the opportunities to show what they know, understand and can do in a variety of contexts, a variety of circumstances and using a range of means of assessment. This variety can only be achieved if, by and large, assessment tasks are kept to the small-scale and manageable. If the opportunities for assessment are fully planned into the teaching and learning, they can take place naturally as the work proceeds and will not distort or take over from the teaching.

3
Recording and reporting National Curriculum history

Profiling and records of achievement

Recording and reporting of pupil performance are obviously an integral part of assessment. Just as we have begun to examine the purpose of assessment and to work towards assessment techniques which can give us more valid and reliable evidence of a pupil's progress, so we have also begun to consider the effectiveness and indeed the fairness of traditional methods of recording and reporting that assessment.

It is interesting that of all recent initiatives in education, that of records of achievement seems to have gained widespread support from within the teaching profession. The RANSC (Records of Achievement National Steering Committee) Report, 1989 was largely welcomed; most local authorities have and are developing their own local records of achievement; indeed, many individual schools are well on the way with piloting and using records of achievement to report pupil performance.

The proposals for a National Record of Achievement clearly demonstrate the Government's intention to use such a record to report National Curriculum attainment at the end of each key stage, at seven, eleven, fourteen and sixteen. However, there is also the flexibility within the NRA (National Record of Achievement) to record achievements in areas other than the solely academic and for the pupil to contribute to the summative document.

The NRA is intended to be a summative document, but one which grows with the pupil throughout his or her whole school career. It can therefore be used as the basis for action planning from one key stage to the next. Nor is the place of ongoing, formative reporting denied, even if it is not absolutely required.

It is clear from many recent developments within LEAs that the formative record of achievement can fit within the National Record of Achievement and can be used, both to record National Curriculum attainment and as a current, agreed statement between pupil and teacher about what has been achieved, what now needs to be addressed and an action plan to allow such progression to take place.

The RANSC initiative concentrated on the general, summative document and on the general skills and attitudes identified by the first phase of most LEA pilot schemes, history teachers, with colleagues from other curriculum areas have been required to provide evidence of a pupil's attainment of these general skills and attitudes based on their observations and interactions with pupils in their lessons. The relationship of subject-specific assessment objectives to these general statements has not been satisfactorily addressed, nor has the idea of cross referencing perceptions of the general skills, for example problem solving, between curriculum areas. Criteria for success in problem solving in history may look very different from those put forward by the science faculty.

There remain a number of fundamental issues open to debate. There are no easy answers, but it is as well at least to be aware of the issues.

Pupil negotiation

One of the most contentious areas would seem to be that of pupil self-assessment and pupil negotiation. Many supporters of the profiling movement would argue that this is central and crucial to the philosophy of records of achievement. Pupils must be involved in and engaged in the assessment process so that they can own it and benefit by it. Assessment is no longer to be imposed by the teacher on the pupil and to reflect only the teacher's opinion of the pupil. If assessment is to be for diagnostic purposes, the pupil must be engaged in a dialogue so that she/he can profit from the process and can be helped to develop to her/his full potential.

Among the very real practical considerations is the problem of time. Pupil negotiation and discussion is time consuming, and with growing concerns about the demands on time of the National Curriculum, how far is it likely that more time can be found for tutors to spend with individual pupils?

There is also concern about training for both teachers and pupils in the skills necessary for negotiation. Many teachers find this aspect of profiling difficult and, as yet, little general training has been forthcoming to help teachers to develop strategies whereby they can have a positive dialogue with pupils. Moreover, many pupils find self-assessment difficult and tend at first to make short, generalised and superficial statements about their progress, often taking refuge in clichés or stereotypes or saying what they think the teacher wants them to say. As the RANSC report points out, it is only with practice that pupils learn to develop the analytical and communication skills which enable them to make a positive contribution which both means something and upon which they can act.

Subject-specific profiles

There is also, at present, a difficult relationship between the general summative profile on which RANSC concentrated and which has been developed by most pilot schemes and the subject-specific profile. On the one hand, individual subject areas are required to contribute towards a profile on general cross-curricular skills such as information handling, organisation, problem solving, communication and creative/imaginative, physical/motor, numerical, social skills. On the other hand, different subject areas are also concerned to develop a subject-specific profile which reports progress within the subject. Moreover, this is not simply a matter of the form of reporting. Underlying this debate are fundamental issues about the contribution of an individual curriculum area to the whole school curriculum and the possibility that the emphasis on the general skills and attitudes could undervalue assessment objectives of individual subjects. We are still faced with the basic question; does assessment, recording and reporting of these general competencies mean anything outside the context of subject-specific assessment? Is it possible to make general statement based on evidence drawn from diverse curriculum areas? Has the direction of the records of achievement movement to date in fact distracted us from a more reliable form of assessment because it has largely ignored the subject-specific contexts?

Obviously there must be a whole-school approach to recording and reporting and all departments should contribute towards a general record of achievement. Moreover, it is vital that any subject-specific profile development is carried out within the context of the whole-school record of achievement or else considerable confusion can result. Pupils and parents are likely to receive very confused messages if one subject area is expressing assessment in terms of such organisational skills as 'brings the right equipment to lessons', whereas others are talking about conceptual and methodological progression within that subject!

Profiling and history teaching

Where, then, does this leave history teachers in terms of profiling? History teachers are now being asked to contribute to a general summative profile of cross-curricular skills and attitudes because this facet of profiling is more developed than the subject-specific profile. Many history departments have also been working on subject-specific criteria for pupil profiles and are now looking at the recording and reporting of National Curriculum history. Can this be successfully integrated into a profiling system?

I would argue that a coherent recording and reporting system which builds on the recent experience of profiling and moves towards the integration of National Curriculum reporting must be the most effective way forward; once again, building the lessons learned by recent initiatives and taking them forward.

Recording and reporting National Curriculum history

Now that final Orders for history have been published, the way forward for the history profile is surely through the recording and reporting of attainment measured against the statements of attainment in the attainment targets.

Considerable fears have been expressed that the recording and reporting of attainment for National Curriculum purposes will add yet another burden on teaching time and will lead to an even greater preoccupation with assessment. How are teachers going to find time to do all this assessment and to record and report to parents? What sort of evidence should be kept? What will the record look like? How do we report to parents? Has all the work which has gone into profiling and records of achievement developments been for nothing?

These concerns are understandable but the advent of the National Curriculum should not lead to yet more demands on time over and above what is already required. Nor should the assessment demands distort and detract from the teaching and learning if assessment is planned for and arises out of what is happening in the classroom.

Moreover, just as it is possible, through careful planning to embed assessment in normal classroom activities, so it should be possible to integrate the recording and reporting requirements of the National Curriculum into a record of achievement. It is not a case of yet another system superimposed on what is already in place, but of adapting current recording and reporting procedures into a coherent, rational and manageable system which can inform teachers, parents and pupils.

The nature of a history profile.

What should be the nature of assessment in history? Should the profile be norm-referenced, criterion-referenced, or should the assessment be based on the pupil's self-assessment (ipsative assessment)?

Norm-referencing represents the traditional approach to assessment. A pupil's performance is assessed in comparison with that of his peers. Any statement which gives a pupil a position in class or, at present, a grade at GCSE when it is accepted that a certain percentile will gain a specified grade, is norm-referenced. The whole thrust of the records of achievement movement is away from this approach, in particular the in-built expectation of failure that it engenders in many pupils. However, it must be recognised that parent and employer expectation is still based on the perception that this is the basis of assessment. The question 'How is she doing in comparison with the rest of the class?' is very common.

It is generally recognised that we should be moving towards criterion-referencing. At the inception of GCSE, Sir Keith Joseph called for a move towards criterion-referencing in GCSE in his speech to the North of England Conference, (1984). In response to this demand, the Secondary Examinations Council set up grade-related criteria working parties. The proposals of the grade-related history working party did not gain widespread acceptance and it seems as though the initiative had withered on the vine. However, with the advent of the National Curriculum and the TGAT Report we do now seem to be moving towards criterion-referenced assessment. In effect this is what the statements of attainment are: pupil performance will be assessed against the statements in order to establish which level has been reached. Thus, it would seem that assessment of pupils against stated levels of achievement is the way forward.

It is also important to consider how often and how regularly a pupil should perform at a particular level before it can be said that his/her performance is consistently at that level. The Final Report of the History Working Group makes the point that pupil performance in history is not linear and progression does not always follow a regular pattern (DES, 1990). Since we are engaged in assessing the skills and concepts which make up historical understanding, the context in which these skills and concepts is assessed is of vital importance. Pupil interest and enjoyment in a particular topic can have a marked effect on their seeming understanding of that topic. Moreover, as has already been stated, it is important to ensure that language difficulties and comprehension do not get in the way of historical understanding.

It is therefore important that the profile is arrived at, not through a single assessment at the end of a unit, but by taking the cumulative results of a number of assessment tasks, which arise naturally out of classroom activity, so that the skills and concepts to be assessed are frequently revisited in the course of a year. This approach will also avoid the 'big bang' perception of assessment which causes so much anxiety to pupils and teacher alike and, as has been demonstrated in Chapter 2, will help to make assessment manageable. Assessment tasks do not have to be mammoth exercises which take hours to produce and administer; they can slot naturally and regularly into normal classroom activity. Nor should a formative profile be based on a single assessment – which has been designed specifically for this purpose.

The third possible approach is ipsative assessment: assessing the pupil against his and the teacher's perceptions of his progress. At first, this seems attractive; it avoids intense competition and feelings of failure but it does pose problems of reliability and validity. In particular, there has to be a starting point from which to assess the individual pupil and surely this has to come from some external criteria?

It would seem therefore that we are moving towards criterion-referenced assessment and reporting and that the logic of the subject demands that assessment in history should be based on the concepts and methodology which make up historical understanding. It is however important that reporting both to parents and pupils is done in language which is comprehensible so that we do not replace one set of education jargon with another. Therefore the reporting document should be simple to follow and could well contain a number of ticks in boxes. What is important to remember is that behind the boxes is a considerable amount of work and thought so that teachers can explain to parents how this assessment was reached and what can be done to enable an individual pupil to improve her performance.

Explaining the statements of attainment

If teachers are encountering difficulties when trying to make sense of the statements of attainment, how can we hope to explain them to pupils and to parents? If the attainment targets do reflect the skills and concepts which make up historical understanding and provide the criterion for a history profile, how do we make these accessible to the world outside history teachers?

Clearly, the assessment objectives defined by the attainment targets and the descriptors of progression provided by the statements of attainment do provide the basis from which a history profile can be devised, but, if we want to make any sense at all to parents and pupils, we cannot use the statements in a record of achievement.

The final Order for history is a document designed to be used by professionals, and just as the history study units in the programmes of study are not in themselves schemes of work and lesson plans, so the attainment targets and statements of attainment do not provide a ready-made reporting system.

To make the system work, it must mean something to its audience, and that means that the language of reporting in turn means something to pupils and parents.

Moreover, as should be the case with GCSE, the assessment criteria should not be a mystery to the pupils. Teachers at GCSE in general agree that it is good practice to share their expectations with the pupils. In terms of GCSE, this means sharing the proposed levels mark scheme with the pupils: 'If you wish to reach Level 3, I would expect you to be able to do this'. Despite some initial doubts as to whether this strategy leads candidates unduly, most teachers now agreed that it is good assessment practice to discuss such expectations with their pupils. With sufficiently open-ended tasks, it is surprising how much room for manoeuvre there still is and how diverse are the responses obtained, even though the mark scheme to be used has been discussed in advance!

The same is true for National Curriculum assessment. Pupils have the right to know precisely what is being assessed and what expectations are. Thus, the statement of attainment must be couched in language they can understand so that they can clearly appreciate what is required.

Defining pupil targets

One of the most effective ways of making these general statements meaningful to pupils is to put them in the context of a specific task in a specific study unit.

For example, when studying the Roman Empire, pupils might be given an activity in which they have a range of sources which consider the reasons for the collapse of the Empire. There is no reason why, before they embark on the task, it should not be explained to the pupils that the purpose of the task is to consider *why* the Empire collapsed; that they should seek a range of reasons from the sources; that they should rank order these reasons in order of importance and explain their rank order with reference to the sources. Pupils the teachers knows to be are capable of working at higher levels might be given extension activities in which they are asked to consider how the reasons for the fall of the Roman Empire are linked and interconnected.

These tasks can be readily cross-referenced to Attainment Target 1b), 'understanding causation', and can, by the teacher, be linked to particular statements of attainment so that pupils' responses can offer evidence of attainment which can be measured against a particular level.

The statements of attainment are much more likely to be understood by pupils and indeed their parents if they are defined in the context of particular tasks, rather than attempting to produce a simplified version of the general statements of attainment.

How far the levels themselves should be used as a basis for discussion with pupils is currently a matter for debate. In the first tentative steps towards National Curriculum recording and reporting, some teachers have now abandoned marks and grades and started to record attainment targets and levels on pupils' work. I have considerable reservations about this approach.

Certainly, the meaning of the attainment targets should be explained to both pupils and parents, as should be the general principle of measuring attainment against the statements of attainment. However, until we have had the opportunity to do considerably more moderation of pupils' work and have begun to work towards a shared and common understanding of what these levels might mean in terms of pupils' work, I would hesitate to go public, just yet, if at all before the end of the key stage. Of course, teachers must record the levels achieved for themselves and must be able to produce this evidence if requested. As far as the pupil is concerned, a helpful, diagnostic comment which affirms what has been achieved and indicates what *might* be achieved, is far more helpful and positive, even for the most able pupil.

The other great benefit of these task-specific pupil targets is that they can provide the basis for meaningful pupil statements on the record of achievement. Pupils can be invited to assess their achievements and progress against these specific targets rather than responding to vague statements such as 'the unit of work I enjoyed most was . . .' 'I need to improve in . . .' 'I did well in . . .'

The problem with these statements is that they are too vague and give little help to pupils to respond with anything other than platitudes. What is more, if pupils are aware of a number of targets which might define what is expected in a whole unit or, as in this case, in a relatively small task, this can be the basis of helpful and supportive dialogue with the teacher which can focus on these targets and can be related to what is taking place in the lesson.

Thus, the problem of pupil negotiation and time can to a great extent be overcome by ongoing, naturally supportive teacher/pupil dialogue which arises spontaneously during the lesson.

Reporting to parents

The reporting of National Curriculum attainment to parents can be made compatible with records of achievement if a coherent assessment system is adopted which perceives that:
- what a teacher assesses reflects what is required by the National Curriculum;
- what is assessed is recorded;
- what is recorded provides the basis for an objective and helpful statement to both pupils and parents.

The following case study is an example of how such coherence might be achieved.

Case study: The formative record

Below is a suggestion for a formative record on which progress might be recorded

The following should be noted:
1. The targets are those which have already been discussed with the pupils. Pupils can also record their attainment in terms of National Curriculum attainment targets and levels.
2. The general skills statement: pupils will have been given guidance (probably a printed sheet to be stuck into their books) which explains what is meant be these general skills. These general skills should also be reflected in the contribution made by the history teacher to a summative general record of achievement. Different tasks and activities are likely to focus on a range of general skills.

   For example, a task focused on AT3, (the use and evaluation of sources) which had arisen as a result of a field trip to a local church, might elicit evidence of information handling which might be explained to the pupils as:

   To complete this task successfully you will have to use the following skill: Information Handling. When using this skill you will: carry out research, observe carefully, collect information, record information accurately, present information, use information to make judgments.

   Pupils can then use this guidance to assess their performance against these statements, thus helping them to make the general statement relate to a task they have recently completed.
3. Personal qualities displayed: again an area of self assessment affirmed in the record of achievement, but if the pupil is to make any sort of constructive response s/he must be helped to make it mean something by relating it to something s/he has actually done.
4. The teacher comment: National Curriculum reporting requirements demand that teachers report to parents in writing once a year. This should not be seen as a contradiction to the record of achievement

movement in which the partnership between pupil, teacher and parent should have been affirmed by the opportunity for all to comment. Furthermore, the teacher's written comment should be another way to demystify the statement of attainment.

Levels of attainment do not have to be reported during the key stage although teachers must keep a record of those levels and parents have the right to see that evidence. It may be that the policy of the school is to give interim reports on the levels of attainment although the advice of many LEAs is not to be too categorical about such statements before the end of the key stage. However, what the teacher should be doing is to use the evidence of attainment acquired throughout the school year in which pupil attainment has been measured against the statements of attainment so that a meaningful, helpful and constructive comment can be made rather than a meaningless generalisation. The teacher's record should therefore inform the comment written on the report.

Such reporting can involve pupils and parents as part of the formative process of assessment. It is not necessary to send all such records home to parents. From a practical, administrative point of view, schools are adopting different strategies for moving from the formative to the summative document. It may be that, in the course of the key stage, a formative document is sent home at then end of each unit of work. The division of National Curriculum history into roughly three such study units a year would lend itself to this. It may be that, although a formative record is completed for each unit, a summary sheet of what has been achieved during the year is sent home to parents with an indication of attainment in history, related to the attainment target levels and the statements of attainment but expressed in more general and accessible language so that parents can understand easily what progress their child is making in history and what help and support is being given to encourage that progress. In history, we can be thankful at least for the restraint of the Working Group in proposing only four attainment targets which were reduced to three by the NCC. It is not beyond the bounds of reason to generalise about progress and attainment in history from these attainment targets, even if one of them has three strands!

Fig. 2
The formative record

Formative Record

Name _____   Date _____

Task: _____

_____

Target and Levels Achieved (in a particular study unit or a specific task)

Targets recorded. Levels achieved checked. Attainment target levels achieved identified (if this is school policy).

General skills statement (pupil response)

_____

Personal qualities displayed (pupil response)

_____

My targets for the future

_____

Teacher comment

_____

Parent's comment (if required)

Recording assessment

There is still the apprehension that the National Curriculum will reduce teaching and learning to checklists of ticks in boxes. Assessment opportunities can however be small-scale, planned within normal work and valid as part of the learning process. Nevertheless, the outcomes of that assessment must be recorded. Is this yet again extra work? It might be instead of an existing system: it certainly should not be as well as.

A teacher's mainstay for record-keeping should remain, as it always has been, the markbook. It might, indeed it should, be the case that the nature of the tasks set develops as a result of the National Curriculum and that tasks planned to deliver evidence of National Curriculum attainment.

It might also be that the history department/humanities faculty marking and assessment policy comes in for some scrutiny.

Towards a coherent marking system

As has already been noted, many pupils can be forgiven for being puzzled and confused about assessment. They can be on the receiving end of a picture of marks, grades, levels, supportive comments, tick, crosses and a variety of other symbols. Are we now about to add another set of assessment hieroglyphics with the advent of the National Curriculum? If recording National Curriculum attainment is not going to confuse the issue even further, now is the time to develop a coherent assessment policy in which the criteria for assessment are made completely clear to pupils, parents and fellow teachers.

Now that the National Curriculum has moved us towards criterion-referenced assessment, the criteria have been defined by the attainment targets and statements of attainment. We may not necessarily agree with them, and must hope that they will be subject to revision in the light of experience at a national level. Meanwhile, as a school level, we must try to make them work. What such a system does provide for the first time is a set of criteria which can be explained to pupils and parents. Given such criteria, one is therefore bound to ask, what is the point of marks and grades? What does seven out of ten or B+ actually mean? What does it tell the pupil about his/her achievement?

Furthermore, we are now in a position not only to make supportive comments but also to give constructive ideas to help the pupil to move from one level to the next.

The first step must therefore surely be an assessment audit in which current practice is scrutinised to identify whether such practice can be used to record National Curriculum attainment.

I have already suggested that task-specific levels of response are a useful mechanism to relate context-specific tasks to the general statements of attainment. It is for the teacher to decide whether the task-specific level should be recorded as well as the evidence this affords of National Curriculum attainment. Indeed, I would urge considerable caution in making too many definitive statements about National Curriculum levels attained before such reporting is required.

Pupils' National Curriculum attainment must be reported to parents at the end of each key stage. For history, therefore, the first absolute requirement to report to parents at the end of Key Stage 3 is July, 1994.

What is required is that the attainment targets are regarded as teaching, learning and assessment objectives and are therefore an integral part of the planning process. Teaching and learning activities and assessment tasks should be devised which focus on these attainment targets and which can, if required, be used to acquire evidence of attainment. This evidence should then be recorded by the teacher to be produced as evidence of National Curriculum attainment if requested by the parents during a key stage. Such evidence should also be used as the basis for helpful and constructive comments to parents and pupils and to help to formulate action plans with pupils which can help them to improve their attainment.

This does *not* mean that reports to parents during the key stage should require definitive statements about the attainment target levels achieved. It has already been stated that the statements of attainment must be regarded as tentative and open to interpretation while we test then against the outcomes of pupils' work. It would seem to be rather foolish to make categorical statements about the levels achieved while we are in the early stages of this process. Indeed by 1994 we are likely to be much more familiar with the statements and what they mean in practice and therefore much more confident about making such judgments.

Recording of attainment is a mechanical exercise but the paranoia about 'ticks in boxes' should not take over. What is important is the process by which a particular decision about attainment against a particular level is reached.

Ideally, the pupil should be given the opportunity to visit particular attainment targets and to demonstrate their level of attainment on several occasions throughout the year and in a variety of contexts. The outcomes of such tasks should be recorded but if the tasks are small scale and part of the ongoing work, there is no reason why they should not be recorded in a mark book as conventional marks and grades always have been.

How will such evidence of attainment be aggregated at the end of the key stage? We do not know as yet whether the NCC recommendation of two profile components will be affirmed by SEAC or if Attainment Target 1 will be given extra weighting (although this has been recommended in the KS3 SAT specification). Advice and guidance on such aggregation will come from SEAC before 1994 when teacher assessment of attainment at the end of KS3 will be reported for the first time. In the meantime, since September 1991, teacher assessment should be planned and recorded. The message must therefore be: don't panic about aggregation; concentrate on recording reliable evidence which can inform reporting to parents and guidance to pupils.

Pupils' records are continuous. Ultimately, teachers at KS3 will received pupils who have completed KS2 and help them to progress from the level they have reached. There will need to be systems of transferring records from KS2 to KS3; information technology can come into its own as a means of storage and retrieval of ongoing records, such as the CASS system developed by Humberside.

Remember too that such records must be transferred at the end of each year in KS3 and that, if the teacher changes, the record must continue. Is there a case for rethinking the traditional personal mark book? Some teachers are moving towards a transferable pupil record which can either be stored on a computer or in a hard copy depending on the availability of IT and the confidence of the history teachers in using it! An example of a possible pupil record is given in Figure 3.

Collecting evidence of attainment

Under the National Curriculum teachers are required to keep evidence of a pupil's attainment. It is unlikely that the mark book will be sufficient. A manageable but effective system is needed to provide evidence of pupils' work at particular levels.

Once again we return to the need for a coherent policy towards assessment. If assessment is integral to what is happening in the classroom, the pupil's current workbook or folder will provide considerable continuous evidence of attainment. However, teachers will need to keep sample pieces of work for moderation and standardisation purposes, but no more than is manageable and reasonable; and as with so much else, it must be dependent on teachers' professionalism and judgment as to what provides sufficient evidence without creating a mountain of paper. It is interesting to note that HMI are recommending a jettison system of storing evidence of attainment: once it is clear that the pupil has progresses from one level to the next, evidence of lower levels can be discarded.

Fig. 3
Pupil record sheet

RECORD OF ACHIEVEMENT
HISTORY ATTAINMENT TARGETS 1, 2 AND 3

SCHOOL:
PUPIL'S NAME:
CLASS:

Date	Study unit	AT1: KNOWLEDGE AND UNDERSTANDING OF HISTORY a) Change 1 2 3 4 5 6 7	b) Cause 1 2 3 4 5 6 7	c) Features of past situations 2 3 4 5 6 7	AT2: INTERPRETATIONS OF HISTORY 1 2 3 4 5 6 7	AST3: USE OF HISTORICAL SOURCES 1 2 3 4 5 6 7	COMMENTS

4
Assessment 16–19

The 16–19 curriculum and the place of A and A/S levels within that curriculum is very much to the fore. There is still considerable pressure to regard A levels as the academic 'flagship' and it does seem likely that, for the foreseeable future, they will remain. Furthermore, there is already considerable pressure for change coming from within the subject-specific groups, not least where history is concerned. As a result of current dissatisfaction with A level history, a number of pilot projects have emerged since 1988 which, although there are marked differences, all reflect a common concern about assessment at A level and have proposed a number of common strategies to answer these concerns.

Proposals for 'core skills' at 16–19 first defined by the NCC at the request of the Secretary of State in 1990, seem to have gone very quiet at present. After considerable delay, SEAC is currently drawing up new criteria for A level courses which could have considerable implications for traditional A level syllabuses and which could well draw on the recent experience of initiatives such as the Cambridge History Project, ETHOS, London Syllabus E and the new JMB syllabuses.

With the amount of activity on the 16–19 curriculum currently being undertaken, it seems sensible to confine the discussion in this chapter to assessment, in the context of both the traditional A level and some possible ways forward based on the work of the most recent initiatives in the assessment of history at this level.

From GCSE to A level

The disfunction between GCSE and the demands of A level has caused some concern. The original perception was that since GCSE did not assess such a wide knowledge base as O level and since the essay was not the paramount means of assessment at GCSE, students would be ill-prepared for the demands of A level. In fact, experience of the past two years has demonstrated that although there is indeed a mismatch between GCSE and the demands of the traditional A level, it is not necessarily in those areas where it was anticipated. Furthermore, it is arguable once again that we should draw from good practice at GCSE in order to improve assessment practices post-sixteen.

The perceived knowledge base of GCE O level was never a particularly strong preparation for A level, nor was the O level essay writing style. Indeed, many less strong A level candidates who had gained respectable O level grades used to come to A level with unrealistic expectations because they found it difficult to understand that the analytical essay demanded by A level was a far cry from the largely factual recall approach of O level. Of course, if the able student had acquired a clear and fluent written mostly before embarking on an A level course, this was bound to hold him or her in good stead, but O level essays in themselves contributed little to the demands of A level.

It is true that certainly in the early cohorts of GCSE candidates, there were individuals who gained GCSE grade C who would probably not have gained an O level pass and who embarked on A level and found it very challenging. Certainly, and this is not just as a result of GCSE, the ability range of students embarking on A level history is significantly wider than was once the case. However, the main reasons for the mismatch between GCSE and A level derives from the positive achievements of GCSE.

Good practice at GCSE has involved pupils in active, participatory learning, in problem solving, in investigation. By the time they have completed their GCSE course many students can bring sophisticated skills of source evaluation and analysis and have been encouraged to challenge, to question, to hypothesise – to know with doubt. By contrast, when they embark on A level too often they can find themselves in a passive role, receiving given information, reading books without question and writing essays which are too often elliptical and obscure.

Since 1987 A level history examinations have been required to conform to the common core. All examinations must include some source evaluation, but frequently this has been focused on comprehension rather than evaluation.

Many teachers accept and recognise this but believe there is little that can be done because the amount of content to be covered is so vast that there is no time for problem-solving discovery methods. One solution has been to become more closely associated with one of the new initiatives or to switch to AEB 673, now a fully-fledged syllabus which has seen a substantial increase in candidate numbers since 1988.

It is possible, however, to consider a number of assessment strategies within the context of a traditional A level approach which can build on rather than undermine what should have resulted from GCSE.

Targeted objectives

Assessment at GCSE has encouraged teachers to design assessment tasks which focus on specific assessment objectives much more tightly. Students are therefore used to complete assignments which have defined assessment objectives. Yet when they come to A level, they are given broad essay titles and have little or no idea what is required.

It is possible to break down some of these titles by discussion of key words, but even this is too broad. Teachers will argue that there are no national assessment criteria for A level and no traditional syllabus produces a criteria-based mark scheme. Common practice at A level is to give the students essay titles from past papers so that they can build up expertise in the type of question they will encounter in the examination.

Within these broad titles, however, it is possible to focus on particular assessment objectives. Moreover these objectives can vary from student to student so that each student has an individual focus on a common essay title which addresses her/his particular needs.

For example, in a course on modern European history, students are given the essay title: 'To what extent was Article 231 of the Treaty of Versailles justified in blaming Germany for the outbreak of the First World War?'

After a certain amount of practice, students come to recognise the types of A level question. The 'key word' exercise is useful in that it alerts students to the main areas of emphasis: 'to what extent' signifies that this is an assessment of the origins of the First World War debate and, at the higher levels, an engagement in that debate. But what are the assessment objectives? Students need to be given guidelines about what is going to be assessed and the criteria on which that assessment will be based.

When teachers mark A level essays, the grade given in often highly subjective. Even if one is well versed in devising and using levels mark schemes for GCSE, it is very challenging is not impossible to devise a levels-of-response mark scheme for such a question as this, because it was not intended to be subjected to such treatment! Here is one of the major problems, the questions themselves. Sean Lang, project officer of ETHOS recently published his research findings into questions set at A level which provides evidence of the lack of clarity and intention of many of the questions set in A level examinations (Lang 1990), and yet, unless the teacher takes the unilateral decision to change syllabus, the student must continue to confront such questions. How can she/he be helped?

It is possible to give the task more definition. For example, the objectives could be expressed as:
• the ability to plan a coherent argument;
• the ability to support the plan with relevant evidence;
• the ability to develop a logical argument when writing the essay;
• clarity of expression.

All these objectives are necessary to write a good A level essay. All should be present, but in order to help the student to develop each and every skill, why not focus on each objective individually? Each student will address the same title, but each will know in advance that he or she will be assessed against a specific defined objective and the assessment grade will be given for that particular objective.

Individual students have individual strengths and weaknesses and in this way can be given individual help. By focusing on, say, supporting the argument with relevant evidence, they become aware that that objective has been identified as a weakness and, for this particular task, can concentrate on it. The teacher should ensure that all objectives are addressed, if necessary by directing which assessment objectives will be addressed, but at this stage in the students' education, it should be possible to arrive at the objective to be assessed by negotiation: students should be able to identify what they perceive as objectives on which they want to concentrate.

The contract book

As the profiling movement gains momentum, so more students will become engaged in pupil–teacher negotiation before they are sixteen. The TVE extension has encouraged profiles and records of achievement to be developed post-sixteen. Indeed, with the advent of open sixth forms and individual programmes of study post-sixteen, it would seem an obvious and necessary measure.

If the idea of negotiated assessment objectives is accepted, there needs to be some method of recording and reporting such negotiation. Hence, the contract book. Every assessment is recorded together with the defined assessment objective for that particular assignment. When the task is assessed, the grade and comment is entered in the book. In this way, the student can build up a picture of strengths and weaknesses and can assess her/his own progress over a longer period of time.

The contract book forms the basis of the contract between student and teacher, and as such should be periodically reviewed, say every half term, in a short discussion in which the student and teacher explore the profile which is emerging in the book. It sounds time-consuming but if each A level teacher is allocated a number of personal 'tutees' and spends no more than five to ten minutes discussing the book each half term, it can be done and the results are very positive, both in academic and personal relationship terms.

It should not be necessary to wait for SEAC's publication of assessment objectives at A level before introducing records of achievement for A and A/S level courses. Students should be made aware of the skills and concepts that underpin an A level history course. By the end of the Year 12, it should be possible for both students and teachers to assess progress in such generic skills as note-taking, essay writing and document work, and to relate these to specific subject areas to demonstrate how effectively students are able to deploy their knowledge relevantly and effectively. Above all, the assessment objectives must be clarified for both student and teacher so that they can engage in a contract in which both are aware of the terms and conditions. It is no longer a case of simply doing A level history with a pass or fail grade at the end of the course.

Source evaluation

The common core agreement ensured that all Boards set A level papers which would include source evaluation questions. The varying ways in which this has been done and the degrees of emphasis placed on such exercises varies from Board to Board as does the type of question set. There is however considerable dissatisfaction with the current state of play and a strong belief that the Boards have abided by the letter rather than the spirit of the agreement.

One problem has been the marginalising of document questions to particular areas of the syllabus. Thus some Boards relate the document questions specifically to the depth study whereas others include them on the outline paper but home-in on particular topics for which books of sources are recommended by the Boards. In either case the temptation is to confine source evaluation exercises and preparation to those parts of the syllabus to which they relate, rather than to make such use of documents fundamental to the whole course. The more students work with, read, question and discuss sources, the more easily they will handle any source evaluation question in the examination.

The way forward

To a greater or lesser extent, the new A level history initiatives have already produced assessment frameworks which may well be incorporated in the final criteria. It is interesting to note that, despite the very different structures of the assessment domains in the Cambridge History Project, the key questions in the JMB syllabuses and the broader objectives of 'doing history' which are encapsulated in ETHOS, the commitment to defined assessment objectives and a variety of means of assessment underpins all the recent initiatives. Similarly, the content in the pilot syllabuses has been considerably reduced so that the lottery element is diminished and time is built-in to develop the skills of investigation and enquiry.

Nor has this development been confined to the pilot syllabuses. A number of traditional syllabuses have now published 'defined topics' which guarantee questions in the examination paper on certain stated areas and which will therefore allow for a more coherent course and one that does not depend on question-spotting and broad coverage.

Core skills might be in question, and the idea of credit transfer through modular schemes seems to have been welcomed by the Government although the dilemma of affirming assessment largely through a terminal examination and at the same time wishing to promote modularity has yet to be resolved!

The impact of the National Curriculum must also be taken into account. Ultimately, those students who have followed a course of National Curriculum history and have reached the higher levels by sixteen will be looking for courses which are challenging and which can develop their conceptual and methodological understanding and expertise still further. Are we on the brink of Key Stage 5? The National Curriculum lays down guidelines for the teaching and learning of history 5–16. The impact on the curriculum post-sixteen is bound to be considerable.

References

Colwill, I. and Burns, M., *History Planning and Assessment,* Hodder and Stoughton, 1989

DES, *History for Ages 5 to 16*, HMSO, 1990

Fines, J. *Question Framing at GCSE and A Level*, Historical Association, 1988

Johnstone, A. H., *Meaning Beyond Readability*, SEC, 1988

Lang, S., *A Level History: A Case for Change*, The Historical Association, 1990

NCC, *History: Non-statutory Guidance*, NCC, April 1991

SEAC, *Chief Examiners' Conference: History*, SEAC, 1989

SEC, *Making Ourselves Clearer: Readability in GCSE*, SEC, 1988

SEC/Joint Council Working Party, *Differentiation by Outcome in History*, SEC, May 1988